The Hemmings Motor News Book of
CORVETTES

ISBN 0-917808-37-1
Library of Congress Card Number: 99-067543

One of a series of Hemmings Motor News Collector-Car Books. Other books in the series include:
Hemmings Motor News Book of Chrysler Performance Cars
Hemmings Motor News Book of Mustangs

The Hemmings Motor News Book of

CORVETTES

Editor-In-Chief
Terry Ehrich

Editor
Richard A. Lentinello

Designer
Nancy Bianco

Cover photo by David Gooley: 1955 Corvette

This book compiles driveReports which have appeared in Hemmings Motor News's Special Interest Autos magazine (SIA) over the past 30 years. The editors at Hemmings Motor News express their gratitude to the following writers, photographers, and artists who made this book possible through their many fine contributions to Special Interest Autos magazine:

Robert C. Ackerson	Michael Lamm
Arch Brown	Mike Major
W. O. Clark	Vince Manocchi
Dave Emanuel	Richard Prince
David Gooley	Roy Query
Jeff Godshall	Rich Taylor
Robert Gross	John G. Tennyson
Robert P. Hage	Russ von Sauers
Tim Howley	Walt Woron
J. William Lamm	

We are also grateful to Dave Brownell, Michael Lamm, and Rich Taylor, the editors under whose guidance these driveReports were written and published. We thank General Motors Corporation and Chevrolet Motors Division, who have graciously contributed photographs to Special Interest Autos magazine and this book.

CONTENTS

Special Interest Autos (SIA) magazine's back issues are referred to in this book by issue number. If in stock, copies may be purchased directly from Hemmings Motor News at 800-227-4373 or at www.hemmings.com.

1954 Corvette

CORVETTE NEWS, Chevrolet's magazine for Corvette owners, ran a contest last year to find the oldest Vette still alive. Winner was Ed Thiebaud, a turkey rancher in Fresno, Calif. Ed owns the third Corvette built, plus perhaps the largest vintage Vette collection in the world—27 in all, including one for every year from 1953 through 1963. It's not just coincidence. Ed is founder and president of the Vintage Corvette Club on America.

The fates of Corvettes #1 and #2 aren't known. We originally had hoped to do a drive-Report on #3, but at the time it was in no shape to photograph. We ventured to Fresno and the Thiebaud turkey ranch anyhow, and after looking over Ed's collection decided to take out his immaculate 1954 roadster. That's the car you see here.

For several years after its introduction in 1953, controversy surrounded the Corvette. Was it or was it not a genuine sports car? This question was laid to rest when ROAD & TRACK did its first road test of the Corvette in 1954. That test began:

"Ever since the Chevrolet Corvette was announced over a year ago, there has been much speculation over its competition performance potential. The diehards . . . have been especially loud . . . maintaining that the Corvette is not a genuine dual-purpose sports car, but more of an effete high-speed touring type. Some have been more specific, claiming that nothing from Detroit could possibly be any good—least of all from Chevrolet.

"Furthermore, some people seem to feel that no car based on standard family car components can be much of a sports car. Nothing could be further from the truth, as can readily be shown by mentioning such famous makes as Mercedes, Porsche, Alfa Romeo, Siata, Lancia, Gordini, Talbot, and Jaguar—all of whom at one time or another built rather successful sports cars using a large proportion of major units from mass-produced family . . . automobiles.

"So it is that the only fair approach to the Corvette must be on the basis of its all-around performance comparison to other sports cars, completely ignoring the fact that it happens to stem from the world's largest producer of automobiles."

The 6-cylinder Corvette gives an odd illusion upon acceleration. It doesn't *feel* fast. The slushy 2-speed Powerglide just sits there and churns when you first tromp the gas pedal. The engine sounds like a motorboat, its muffled growl accelerating much faster than the rear tires do. But then suddenly, at around 10 mph, the Powerglide firms up and you feel yourself shoved back in the seat firmly, and from here the car really takes off. The motorboat sound continues, but the car's road speed begins rising in cadence to the steady purr.

ROAD & TRACK recorded a 0-60 time of 11.0 second which, for the day, wasn't half bad. As R&T said, "The Corvette will give any sports car of comparable power and weight a real race between 20 and 90 mph." And R&T's fastest timed 1-way run in 1954 was 107.1 mph.

In the handling department, we felt that Ed's roadster turned out to be remarkably stable and predictable. It leaned hardly at all through corners. Yet its ride was typically American "boulevard," as opposed to, say, the XK-120's much firmer and jouncier ride. Chevrolet achieved an admirable compromise between ride and handling, especially since their engineers didn't have independent rear axles to work with.

The vintage Corvette isn't at all noisy. With the top down, it's hard to carry on a normal conversation at 60 mph, but with it up, you hear nothing but the soft murmur of the twin exhausts—otherwise the car is very well insulated. The top doesn't drum, and there are no rattles. Driving stance feels great: a near-vertical steering wheel, nicely spaced pedals, everything easy to reach and read. Brakes aren't spectacular, but they're surely up to their job. R&T reported that they were little affected by water.

The early Vette arrived at a time when amateur sports car racing enjoyed great weekend popularity. People who owned Jags and Porsches and Healeys drove their cars on the street during the week and then dodged haybales at airports on Sundays. Here's where the 1953-4 Corvette got left in the parking lot, because with Powerglide the only transmission available, plus passenger-car brakes, it wasn't really suited to road racing. That's another reason so many purists merely smiled at the mention of the Corvette name.

The Corvette, like Cadillac's Eldorado Brougham, began life as a styling exercise and Motorama show car. It started out as a series of doodles by Harley Earl, GM's chief of styling, in about 1950. Earl's son was entering college around that time, and Earl might have been daydreaming about a nice sportster for college kids. The wealthier freshmen in his son's class were driving new XK Jags and MGs.

Earl's sketches began to take a more positive shape in 1951 as a medium-sized sports car with a V-8 engine. This idea went along for several months in complete secrecy, mostly because there was no reason to tell anyone about it. One of the first people Earl showed his drawings to was Bob McLean, a young sports car enthusiast Earl had recently hired as a designer-engineer. McLean held twin degrees from Cal Tech, one in engineering and one in design.

McLean got interested and laid out several full-sized side views, showing major components in place. At the time, the Jaguar XK-120 being all the rage, McLean roughed in a 6-cylinder engine, shoving it back tightly against the firewall. He also placed the driver low and toward the rear. In styling, though, the car looked more like the Mercedes 300-SL, introduced in 1952 as a pure racing car.

At this point, which takes us to around the end of 1951, Earl's roadster still wasn't anything more than blue sky. No one had the slightest inkling that it would ever go into production. Harley Earl, though, and his staff decided to build a plaster mockup to see what it looked like in the round.

Earl and everyone else who saw it liked the car so much that Earl decided to hold a special showing. The audience consisted of four people—Earl, GM president Harlow Curtice, Chevy general manager T.H. Keating, and Chevrolet chief engineer Ed Cole.

As it happened, Chevrolet Div. needed an entry for the 1953 GM Motorama. The division had been caught short at previous shows. (Motoramas, for those who don't know, were big, elaborate car shows held by General Motors in major cities during the 1950s. These shows combined the debut of each year's regular GM lines, spiced with futuristic dream cars, plus leggy chorus girls in song and dance.) Harley Earl's roadster seemed just the thing for Chevy, and to make it more interesting, Ed Cole, who's now GM president, said he'd provide engineering talent to make the car more than just a body shell. He'd make the thing run.

Harley Earl's original plan called for an *inexpensive* sports car—to appeal to people of college age who couldn't afford Jags and MGs. He initially aimed toward a base price of $1000. As the car became Motorama material, since no one dreamed even then that it would go into production, it began to take on refinements, thus a higher price. But Earl fought to keep it as simple and inexpensive as possible, and as Motorama showsters went, this was to be one of the cheapest.

Engineers assigned to the project included Bob McLean, Vince Kaptur Sr., Ed Cole, and Maurice Olley—some of the very best talent in the nation. To keep costs down, they started with a 1953 Chevrolet passenger-car frame and whacked 13 inches out of its wheelbase—down to 102 inches. The trusty old (*see* Twin 1932 Chevys, *SIA, Nov. 1970*) Blue Flame 6 got three sidedraft Carter carbs, solid lifters, a wilder cam, and twin exhausts. To make the engine fit beneath the low hood, sidedraft carbs became a must. The engineers also had to add a detached top tank to the radiator, lower the rocker cover, and develop a new casting for the front of the block.

With its hop-up modifications, the amply chromed Chevy 6 brought forth 150 bhp from 235.5 cid. This powerplant was moved back in the frame seven inches, fully behind the front suspension which, in turn, put the driver back so far he could buff his fingernails on the rear

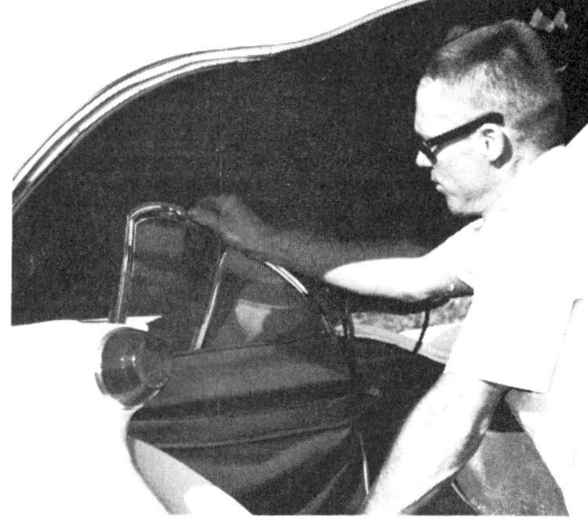

Driving Around With Walt Woron

*Walt Woron, the man who made **Motor Trend** and now generally acknowledged to be the dean of American automotive editors, reminisces about his initial reactions to the first Corvette. That's Walt behind the wheel in the photo above (taken at the GM Proving Grounds in 1953), with Mauri Rose beside him.*

MY FIRST introduction to the 1953 Corvette was in the summer of 1953 in Detroit and was what I called at the time a "pleasant, but *pleasant* surprise." Writing in MT about Chevy's new offering, I described it as having "go from a traffic light, punch at high speeds, an uncanny ability to stay flat around sharp turns, a solid ride [with] eye appeal as well." It was no "competition sports car" but one that "could be made so with suitable modifications."

History has proved me right, for within the next year I had personal experience with a rash of modified Corvettes. But that's another story.

To a purist like me (I owned a 1948 MG-TC at the time), the idea of an automatic transmission in a sports car was unthinkable, even if the selector lever was next to the driveshaft tunnel. Later, with 3-time Indy winner Mauri Rose demonstrating his effortless technique of downshifting for braking and accelerating out of corners, I had to admit grudgingly that an automatic could be at home in a sports car.

Taking the Corvette around GM's Ride & Handling course, the Corvette's suspension seemed good enough to not only keep it flat in the corners, but it stuck better than some foreign sports cars of the time. Steering response, even with a not-so-fast 16:1 ratio, also rated high. Mauri showed me how stable the car really was by taking some sweeping bends at 70-75 mph that I felt at the time "would have flipped a stock Chevy into the bushes." Yes, I guess you'd say I was impressed.   —**Walt Woron**

Tach stands at center of complete dash array. Red warning light under speedo plugs hole left when trans selector was moved to floor tunnel.

Ed Thiebaud's "museum" includes 27 solid-axle Vettes, including the 3rd one built. Ed stores as many as possible in this air-tight room.

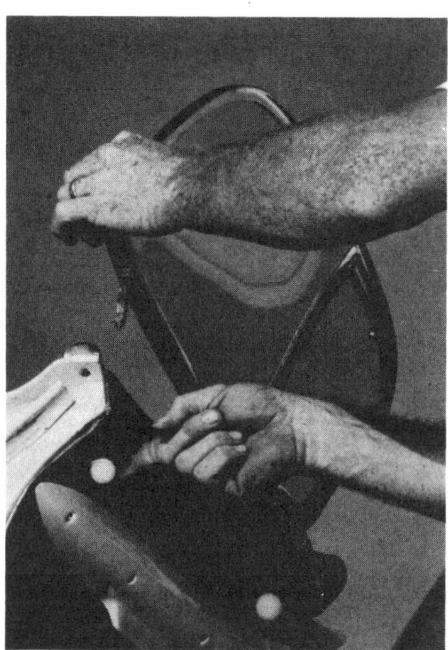

With no glovebox in dash, deep door bin holds all smaller, loose items. There's one on each side.

Rigid sidecurtains plug into door, stow in special bag in the trunk. Other ball is door handle.

Triple sidedraft Carters dominate engine. Chromed radiator header tank flanks low-profile rocker cover. Chromed ignition shield keeps plugs from broadcasting themselves through fiberglass body.

1954 Corvette

premium wide whites—standard equipment.

Maurice Olley, who'd cut his teeth at Rolls-Royce and Cadillac, set up the Corvette's suspension, placing the rear leaf springs far outboard and angling them inward at their fronts to give lots of roll understeer. Front suspension remained stock Chevy, with only a stabilizer bar added.

Now, just on the eve of the 1953 Motorama circuit (in late 1952), Harley Earl put the finishing touches on his car's styling. It still didn't have a name, but "Corvair" was being considered. Fiberglass was the logical body material, being much easier and cheaper to work with than steel for a show car. As it turned out, three cars were finally built—a roadster called the Corvette, a fastback called "Corvair," and a station wagon dubbed "Nomad."

Earl originally envisioned plexiglas headlight covers to fit the Corvette's front fender contour. These were rejected, though, when someone in management suggested they would catch mud. So Earl tried eggcrate aluminum headlamp grilles made up of strips of flat stock. Those looked awful, thus finally he settled on the chrome fencing-mask mesh. At one point, too, someone mentioned putting a spare tire on the trunk, continental style, but Earl soon quashed that.

In his futile quest to keep the Corvette inexpensive, Earl tried to hold all elements to their basic essentials: sidecurtains instead of roll-up windows, no outside door handles, minimal chrome, and no great creature comforts. Of course, that was fine for a sports car.

The Corvette prototype, its name still not confirmed and carrying only the word *Chevrolet* on its front fenders, proved the absolute hit of the 1953 Motorama. People flocked around it. The press carried its picture into every home (not only the motoring press but general-interest publications as well). Response was immediate and enthusiastic enough to help convince Chevrolet to go into limited production.

Vince Kaptur, an engineer on Earl's staff, recalls that some of the Motorama audience most interested in the roadster were the people from Ford. Ford engineers came to the New York show and literally fell all over the Corvette, "Corvair," and "Nomad," measuring every possible dimension. There's little doubt that they did this to compare specs with their

1954 Corvette

own Thunderbird, which was going into its final development phases at the time.

Chevrolet's decision to produce the Corvette roadster was based partly on public response then, but also to counter the 2-seater T-Bird threat and the rumored upcoming fiberglass Kaiser-Darrin. Other carmakers had similar sporty cars either in production or in the works—Nash-Healey, Hudson Italia, Muntz Jet, the Studebaker Starliner coupe, Crosley Hot Shot, etc. In addition, several backyard bodymakers were turning out rather successful fiberglass shells—Devin, Glaspar, Woodhill. And as a final decision reinforcement, imported sports cars such as Jaguar, Porsche, and MG were selling like crazy.

Originally, the Corvette was supposed to have a steel body in production form, but there wasn't time to tool for one. So the decision was made to go with fiberglass. Chevrolet set up a special assembly line at its Flint, Michigan, plant, and the first production Corvette rolled out of the factory in late September 1953. Chevrolet initially hoped to build 1,000 a month during 1954, and since the Flint line couldn't handle that many, production was moved to St. Louis for the 1954 and later runs.

Powerglide was that initial series' only available transmission. A last-minute decision to use a floor gearshift lever left a round hole in the dash where the column had poked through. Someone plugged the hole with a "handbrake on" warning light. Management had also wanted to add exterior door handles and roll-up windows, but it was too late. So the sidecurtains became heavy, rigid plastic with openable vent panes.

By the time, though, that the first Corvette hit the street, its price had shot up way beyond Earl's $1,000 projection. At a time when you could buy a new Bel Air sport coupe for $1,761 f.o.b., the Corvette came out with a base of $3,440.

Most Vettes in that initial 1953 run went to GM bigwigs and high-volume dealers. Three hundred cars were built during the latter part of 1953, all of them polo white (leading many people to believe that white was the only color fiberglass came in). In its second production year, 1954, Chevrolet built 3,625 Corvettes. These came in additional colors but were completely unchanged in design.

Chevrolet tossed a lot of cash into early ads and promotion and thus lost, it's said, an undisclosed but very substantial dollar amount on every new Corvette sold. In fact, rumor has it that Corvettes still lose money today, but that's not so. According to Chevrolet, Corvettes started making money in 1958 and have been doing so ever since.

For 1955, while styling remained essentially the same, the lightweight Chevy V-8 became available for the first time, as did a manual gearbox and still more color choices. That year, too, Corvette got to be a road-raced car, and it did nicely. In later years it did better than nicely, although it never became a tremendous threat in professional competition. ᐁ

Our thanks to Ed Thiebaud, Pres., Vintage Corvette Club of America, 2359 W. Adams, Fresno, CA 93706; to Road & Track *magazine;* Corvette News; *and Chevrolet Motor Division.*

SPECIFICATIONS

1954 Corvette 2-passenger roadster

Price when new . . . . $3440 f.o.b. Detroit (1954).

Current valuation . . . . Xlnt. $4700; gd. $2130.

ENGINE

Type	Ohv 6, in-line, water-cooled, cast-iron block, 4 mains.
Bore & stroke	3.56 x 3.94 in.
Displacement	235.5 cu. in. (3861cc).
Max. bhp @ rpm	150 @ 4200
Max. torque @ rpm	223 @ 2400.
Compression ratio	8.0:1.
Induction system	3 sidedraft Carter carbs, mechanical fuel pump.
Exhaust system	Split cast-iron manifolds, twin mufflers & exhaust pipes.
Electrical system	6-volt battery/coil, shielded ignition (Delco-Remy).

CLUTCH

Type	None.

TRANSMISSION

Type	Powerglide 2-speed automatic with torque converter.
Ratios: lst	3.82:1.
2nd	1.00:1.
Reverse	3.82:1.

DIFFERENTIAL

Type	Hotchkiss, spiral-bevel gears.
Ratio	3.55:1.
Drive axles	Semi-floating.

STEERING

Type	Semi-irreversible worm & sector.
Turns lock to lock	3.7.
Ratio	16:1.
Turn circle	36.75 ft.

BRAKES

Type	4-wheel drums, hydraulic, internal expanding.
Drum diameter	11.0 in.
Effective lining area	154.4 sq. in.

CHASSIS & BODY

Frame	Box-girder steel, X-member, double dropped.
Body	Laminated fiberglass-reinforced plastic.
Body style	2-door, 2-passenger roadster, manual top, plastic sidecurtains.

SUSPENSION

Front	Independent, unequal A-arms, coil springs, stabilizer bar, tubular hydraulic shock absorbers.
Rear	Longitudinal leaf springs, hydraulic shock absorbers.
Tires	6.70 x 15 4-ply tube type, wide whitewalls.
Wheels	Drop-center rim, pressed steel bolt-ons.

WEIGHTS & MEASURES

Wheelbase	102.0 in.
Overall length	167.0 in.
Overall height	51.25 in.
Overall width	72.24 in.
Front & rear tread	57.0/59.0 in.
Ground clearance	6.0 in.
Curb weight	2850 lb.

CAPACITIES

Crankcase	5 qt.
Cooling system	17.75 qt.
Gas tank	17.25 gal.

PERFORMANCE (from **Road & Track,** June, 1954)

0-30 mph	3.7 sec.
0-40 mph	5.3 sec.
0-50 mph	7.7 sec.
0-60 mph	11.0 sec.
0-70 mph	14.8 sec.
0-80 mph	19.5 sec.
Standing ¼ mile	17.9 sec.
Fastest top-speed run	107.1 mph.

FUEL CONSUMPTION

Best	20-21 mpg.
Average	14-18 mpg.

* Courtesy **Antique Automobile Appraisal.**

SIA comparisonReport

by Arch Brown
photos by Vince Manocchi

NOT since the days of the Stutz Bearcat and the Mercer Raceabout had Americans shown much interest in sports cars. But then, in the years just after World War II the British came along and changed all that. First there was the quaint little MG-TC. Others followed, but the next big splash came with the introduction of the sensational Jaguar XK-120. (See *SIA* #65.)

Evidently this was the point at which the American automobile industry began to sit up and take notice. For unlike the diminutive MG, the Jag came fairly close to the dimensions and displacement with which US manufacturers were familiar. Not only did there appear to be a potential profit in this segment of the business, but — much more important — a flashy sports car couldn't possibly hurt the sales of bread-and-butter sedans.

It was Nash, surprisingly enough, that was the first to market an American sports car — or rather, an American-*powered* sports car; for the Nash-Healey (see *SIA* #71) was really an international hybrid. Sales were something less than sensational, doubtless due to the car's very stiff price, but a first-in-class (second overall) at Le Mans in 1952 and assorted other triumphs in competitive events gave Nash a dandy shot of publicity.

Not surprisingly, then, two more American manufacturers followed suit: Chevrolet in 1953, two years after the Nash-Healey's debut, and Kaiser early the following year. The newcomers were, of course, the Chevrolet Corvette and the Kaiser-Darrin.

Once having determined to build a sports car, the men at Chevrolet set about their task in a hurry. From the time the first plaster model was displayed until the fiberglass-bodied Corvettes began to come off the production line on June 30, 1953, less than 13 months had elapsed!

The Corvette represented General Motors' first use of fiberglass in a production automobile. Ed Cole, who in considerable measure was responsible for the sports car's rapid development, estimated that the fiberglass shell reduced the Corvette's weight by some 300 pounds compared to the heft of a steel-bodied car of the same design. More important for a limited-production automobile, it saved about $4 million in tooling costs.

In the course of the Corvette's development, General Motors experimented with the possibility of impregnating the plastic with color, in order to eliminate the need for paint. Not only would such a procedure, if successful, have effected a further cost-saving, but the problem of chipping paint, common to all lacquered and enameled surfaces, would have been eliminated. In the end, however, the effort was abandoned. The impregnated color failed to produce the deep, brilliant luster of a painted surface.

Apart from its body, the Corvette employed Chevrolet components almost exclusively, in either stock or modified form. Power for the early Corvettes came from a jazzed-up version of Chevy's hoary "stovebolt six." Modifications to that venerable engine included an extra squeeze to the compression ratio (8.0 instead of 7.5), a high-lift camshaft, extra heavy valve springs and mechanical tappets, a split exhaust and three Carter sidedraft carburetors. Horsepower was thus raised from the stock Chevrolet's modest 125 (as fitted to Powerglide-equipped cars) to a lively 150 (and to 155 in 1954, thanks to a further revision of the camshaft.) This was done, it must be confessed, at some sacrifice in smoothness.

In an effort to broaden the Corvette's market appeal, an automatic transmission was fitted — a beefed-up version of the familiar, two-speed Powerglide. In retrospect, it appears that Chevrolet made a serious mistake in not offering Corvette customers the option of a stick shift, preferably a four-speed, for dyed-in-the-wool sports-car fans tended to look upon the slush box with disdain, and it colored (or perhaps *discolored*) their overall impression of the car. The

1954 Chevrolet Corvette vs. Kaiser Darrin

Comparative Specifications
1954 Chevrolet Corvette and Kaiser Darrin

	CORVETTE	DARRIN
Price (f.o.b. factory w/std. equip.)	$3,523	$3,668
Engine — type	ohv L-6	F-head L-6
Bore x stroke	3.5625 x 3.9375	3.125 x 3.5
Displacement	235.5 cubic inches	161 cubic inches
Compression ratio	8.0:1	7.6:1
Bhp @ rpm	155 @ 4,200	90 @ 4,200
Torque @ rpm	223 @ 2,400	135 @ 1,600
Carburetor	Triple sidedraft	Single downdraft
Electrical system	6-volt	6-volt
Clutch — type	—	Single plate
Diameter	—	8.5 inches
Transmission — type	Torque converter with gears	3-speed selective (overdrive optional)
Ratios	1.82:1/1.00:1	2.605:1/1.630:1/1.000:1
Overdrive ratio	—	0.7:1
Final drive — type	Hypoid	Hypoid
Ratio	3.55:1	4.10:1 (4.55:1 w/overdrive)
Steering — type	Worm and sector	Worm and roller
Ratio	16.0:1	15.5:1
Turn circle	39 feet	35 feet
Turns lock to lock	3.9	2.75
Brakes — type	4-wheel hydraulic	4-wheel hydraulic
Drum diameter	11 inches	11 inches
Lining area	158 square inches	176 square inches
Frame	Box section w/ x-member	Reinforced box type
Body construction	Fiberglass	Fiberglass
Front suspension	Independent coil spring	Independent coil spring
Rear suspension	Semi-elliptic leaf springs	Semi-elliptic leaf springs
Shipping weight	2,705 pounds	2,175 pounds
Wheelbase	102 inches	100 inches
Overall length	167 inches	184 inches
Overall width	72.24 inches	67.56 inches
Overall height (top up)	51.5 inches	50.81 inches
Ground clearance	6 inches	7 inches
Tire size	6.70 x 15	5.90 x 15
Tread (front/rear)	57 inches/59 inches	54 inches/54 inches
Capacities: crankcase	5 quarts (6 w/filter)	5 quarts
Cooling system	18.25 quarts	12 quarts
Fuel tank	17.25 gallons	13 gallons
Performance: 0-30 mph	4.3 seconds	4.4 seconds
0-60 mph	11.6 seconds	16.25 seconds
Standing quarter mile	16.4 seconds	19.8 seconds
Top speed	105 mph	95.5 mph
Production (model year)	3,640	435
Horsepower per c.i.d.	.658	.559
Pounds per horsepower	17.5	24.2
Pounds per c.i.d.	11.5	13.5

comparisonReport

oversight was corrected in later years, of course; a three-speed manual gearbox became available in 1956 and a four-speed a year later.

Certain relatively minor yet critical modifications were made to the stock Chevrolet suspension for the Corvette application. Front coil springs were calibrated to take account of the Corvette's relatively light weight; rear springs were reduced from seven leaves to four, and a large-diameter stabilizer bar stiffened the roll. The Corvette's low center of gravity — 18 inches above the ground — also contributed to a reduced roll angle in cornering. Weight distribution, with two people aboard, was about 52/48.

Hotchkiss drive was substituted for Chevy's traditional torque tube, a change necessitated by the Corvette's bobtail chassis. (Its wheelbase, at 102 inches, was more than a foot shorter than that of the standard Chevrolet.) Steering, in typical Chevrolet fashion, was of the worm-and-sector variety, and an oversized master cylinder was employed for the Corvette's brakes.

The Kaiser-Darrin, aimed at the same market segment as the Corvette (and intended, no doubt, as a last-ditch attempt to breathe life into Henry Kaiser's rapidly expiring automotive enterprise) made even greater use than its rival of standard, in-house components.

Conceived by famed designer Howard "Dutch" Darrin, who had already been responsible for the design of both the first and second generation Kaiser sedans, the prototype sports car had

*Left: Darrin is highly individualistic in its styling approach and remains one of the most memorable cars to hit the roads during the fifties. **Below:** Corvette's appearance remained unchanged from its inaugural year of 1953. **Bottom left:** Darrin's taillamp was adopted from '54 Kaiser sedans. **Bottom right:** Corvette used its own specially styled taillamps.*

been constructed in Darrin's own Santa Monica, California, shop. Supposedly Henry Kaiser was upset, initially, at what he presumed to be the unauthorized expenditure of his company's dwindling funds, and he disclaimed any interest in producing the sleek little machine. Two factors contributed to his eventual acceptance of the Kaiser-Darrin. The first of these was Kaiser's realization that it had been developed at Darrin's expense and not his own. And the second was Mrs. Kaiser's enthusiastic approval of the new car.

Again, as with the Corvette, the Kaiser-Darrin's gestation period was a short one. From the time Dutch Darrin first displayed the prototype to Mr. and Mrs. Kaiser until the day the little car became available to the public in December 1953, a scant 13 months had passed — coincidentally, the same development time as that of the Corvette. (The comparison is not quite fair, of course. Kaiser had started with a running prototype, while Chevrolet commenced with merely a plaster mock-up.)

The Kaiser-Darrin's chassis was that of the diminutive Henry J. In this instance, little modification was required because the 100-inch wheelbase was already the correct length for Darrin's purposes. The Henry J's driveline was entirely suitable, too; spring rates were properly calibrated for this new application, and other components were equally appropriate. Darrin had employed the L-head, six-cylinder Henry J engine for his prototype car, but Kaiser's 1953 acquisition of Willys made available the latter's superior F-head six for use in the production units.

But if the mechanical components were conventional, the Kaiser-Darrin's body structure was not. For an organization as closely tied to the steel industry as Kaiser to be producing a fiberglass-bodied automobile has a certain irony to it, yet the use of this new type of body construction was dictated by the same logic that prevailed at Chevrolet.

Darrin, however, added an interesting fillip of his own design. Dutch had long been fascinated with the concept of sliding doors as an alternative to the conventional swing-out variety. In a low-slung automobile such as the Kaiser-Darrin, the problem of striking the curb upon opening the door was thus eliminated, and parking in tight spaces was facilitated as well. The concept was a daring one, but the results — as we shall see presently — were mixed.

In addition to the engine switch, two important changes in the prototype design were made before the Kaiser-Darrin reached production. The first of these was the one-piece windshield, taking the place of the split design on the original car. The alteration was a distinct improvement. The other change, however, infuriated the volatile Mr. Darrin: The front fender line was lifted by several inches, in order to meet the minimum headlight-height laws then in effect in many states. Dutch thought the change distorted the Kaiser-Darrin's profile, and to a degree he was correct; his original design really does seem to have the edge over the configuration that was adopted for production.

Sales predictions emanating from both Chevrolet and Kaiser for their new sport models were wildly optimistic. Chevrolet anticipated producing 1,000 Corvettes a month by 1954; in fact, they turned out less than a third of that number. Kaiser let it be known that the first year's output of their little sports car would be 2,000 units. In the end, as best the figure can be determined, only 435 were built — and many of those failed to sell. Darrin himself purchased something like 50 of the leftover cars in

11

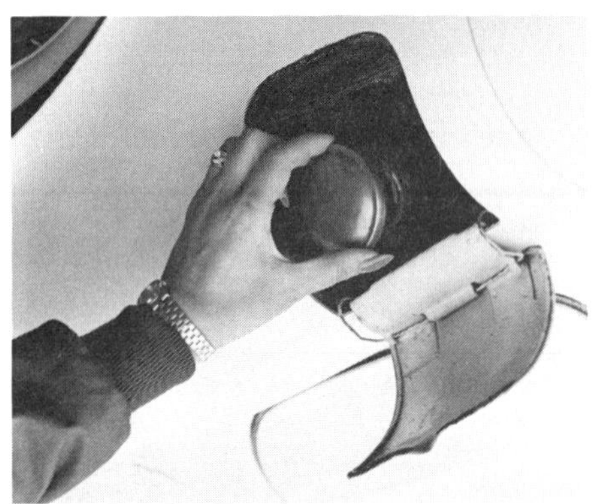

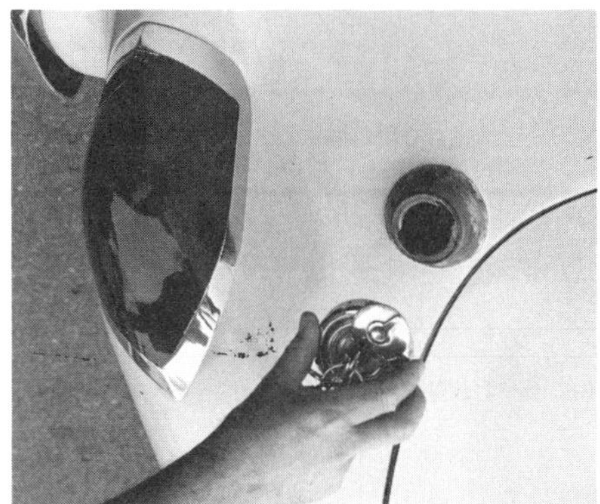

comparisonReport

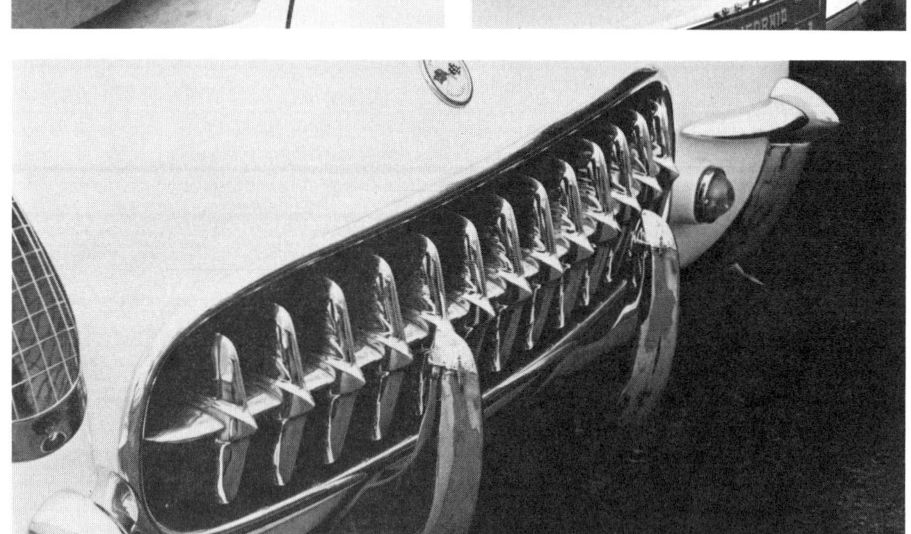

1956, and set about to make them into really sizzling performers. In some instances he fitted the McCulloch supercharger to the Willys engine, raising its horsepower output by half, from 90 to 135. It was soon learned that driving this hot little number flat-out was not, to put the matter delicately, conducive to engine longevity!

Howard Darrin's other power option in the re-worked cars was even more startling: He replaced the little Willys six with a 285-horsepower Cadillac V-8! The result, as Rich Taylor has observed, was "more thrills than the flimsy Henry J chassis could stand."

Production of the Kaiser-Darrin came to a halt after only nine short months. In no small measure, its troubles appear to have stemmed from the public's lack of confidence in Kaiser's future as a producer of motorcars. The doubts were well founded; within a year of the demise of the little sports car, Kaiser's North American automobile operations shut down altogether.

Had it not been for the enormous resources of General Motors and the determination of Ed Cole, the Corvette might not have lasted much longer than the Kaiser-Darrin. After a disappointing start in 1953-54, sales of Chevy's sports

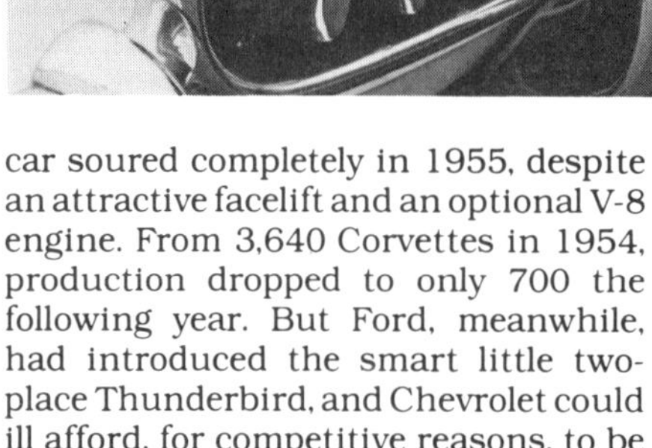

car soured completely in 1955, despite an attractive facelift and an optional V-8 engine. From 3,640 Corvettes in 1954, production dropped to only 700 the following year. But Ford, meanwhile, had introduced the smart little two-place Thunderbird, and Chevrolet could ill afford, for competitive reasons, to be without a "personal" car of its own.

By this time Zora Arkus-Duntov had become, in effect, the Corvette's chief engineer, and for the 1956 model he made a number of important changes to the chassis. High-speed stability was increased, rear wheel lift was reduced, and constant steering response was

achieved in all types of driving. Duntov succinctly summarized the result: "The car goes where it is pointed!"

To this revised chassis was mated Chevrolet's excellent 265 V-8 in either of two states of tune, producing 210 or 225 horsepower, and a three-speed manual transmission was standard issue. The Corvette was beginning to come into its own! Soon, new performance records began to be posted: zero to 60 in 7.5 seconds, and a top speed of more than 150 miles an hour at Daytona Beach, Arkus-Duntov himself at the wheel.

Sales took off. From 1955's nadir of only 700 cars, production shot ahead to

3,467 in 1956; 6,339 in 1957; and an amazing 9,168 in the recession year of 1958 when everyone else — Rambler excepted — was experiencing a severe sales decline. After a wobbly start, the Corvette had made for itself a secure place in the scheme of things at GM.

In preparing this comparisonReport we were privileged to have the use of a Kaiser-Darrin belonging to John Fawcett, of La Jolla, California, and a Corvette owned by pianist-songwriter Richard Carpenter. Both are 1954 models, and both are in near-mint condition. Richard happened to be on tour in Europe at the time of our visit, so Jim Ogle brought the Corvette to La Jolla for our photo session.

The two cars make an interesting contrast. They may have been aimed at the same market segment, but they represent widely divergent concepts of what a sports (or sports-oriented) automobile ought to be.

We drove the Kaiser-Darrin first, and for a brief moment we wondered if we'd be able to manage the assignment. The doors slide forward easily into the fenders, but they don't slide very far. The space between the door frame and the seat was not designed to readily admit a pair of size twelves. Nor does the cockpit comfortably accommodate a driver who — like this one — measures six-feet-two and weighs in at 200 pounds. It was a tight squeeze, and once in place we found the steering wheel resting lightly on our legs. Not enough, really, to interfere with our control of the car, but not particularly comfortable, either.

The seat is very low. Legs are in a straight-out position, not unusual for a car of this type, and not at all uncomfortable. Lateral support is minimal, however, and support to the lower back also leaves something to be desired.

The padded dashboard includes a full set of instruments, including a tach-

ometer, all of them large and well-arranged for readability. There's no package compartment in the dash, however — no place at all to stow maps and small packages. The top appears to be snug. A vacuum is actually created, resulting in cigarette smoke being sucked quickly out of the passenger compartment. We're told by John Fawcett, however, that in a rainstorm the Darrin leaks. Badly — and with no apparent remedy available.

We said the doors slide easily, and so they do — *provided the tracks are kept scrupulously clean*. It's a constant, bothersome but absolutely necessary

maintenance chore with the Kaiser-Darrin. And by the way, there are no inside door handles. One reaches over the door to the outside to release the sliding portal.

The clutch is stiff, as befits a sports-oriented automobile. The floor shift feels a little sloppy and throws are long, but fast shifts are comparatively easy nevertheless. Acceleration is brisk as the car takes off from rest, but the curve quickly flattens out. There's adequate punch for normal passing maneuvers at highway speeds, but it's just that: adequate, not exciting.

The car's performance is smooth,

Top: Both cars have quite distinctive rear-end styling. Darrin would have to be considered more avant garde of the two.
Above and above right: *Corvette has the definite edge over the Darrin in both appearance and power output in the engine compartment.* ***Right:*** *Corvette's dual air cleaner setup for its triple carbs.*

comparisonReport

however, and the ride isn't bad for a short-wheelbase automobile. There's no strain on the engine at any sane speed, particularly with the overdrive engaged. We didn't open it up to full-bore, but according to Wilbur Shaw's 1954 road test, even wide open the tachometer registers just 5,700 rpm. There is no red line, but our guess is that the little F-head could stand that pace with no more than minimal distress.

The Kaiser-Darrin's brakes, borrowed from the full-sized Kaiser sedan, are huge for a vehicle of this weight, and they are very, very good. Nor is there any appreciable "nosedive," even when the binders are applied hard.

Steering is easy, fairly light, and neither especially fast nor slow. But like some other cars of the Darrin's vintage, irregularities in the road are transmitted rather too faithfully to the driver's hands.

This particular car has been driven only 43,000 miles. By a long-shot coincidence, its original owner's son was the "steady" boyfriend of the present owner's daughter during their college days, some years ago — long before John acquired the car. It's a nice restoration from a very decent original car, finished off with an excellent paint job applied for John Fawcett by Buddy Holly.

The long hood that is one of the Darrin's major styling features provides plenty of room for the engine; accessibility is excellent. There's a neat "hatch cover" to hide the top when it is folded away. Erect, it can be held in landau position if desired, or fully unfolded for protection against the elements. And the trunk is roomier than we expected, given the car's short-deck configuration.

Moving over to Richard Carpenter's Corvette, we expected something quite different from the Kaiser-Darrin, and in most respects that's just what we got. One similarity, however, lay in the cramped driving quarters. It's easier to board than the Darrin, despite the windshield's rather nasty "dogleg," but leg room is still scant. Seats are more supportive than those of the Darrin, and the driving position is good — except that, once again, we found the steering wheel resting on our lap. And this one too, according to Jim Ogle, ships water in the rain.

The engine is vastly more powerful than the Kaiser-Darrin's, but not quite as civilized. It didn't really smooth out, in fact, until our speed got up to 30 or 35. From that point on, it was as docile as a kitten. We were a little surprised at the roughness, but perhaps we shouldn't have been. After all, Chevy engineers had coaxed an extra 30 horses — 24 percent — out of the aging six.

Cornering ability is superior to that of the Kaiser-Darrin, though no match for that of the later Corvettes. Steering, though easy, seems a bit too slow, at 3.9 turns lock-to-lock. But it is fairly precise and less prone than the Darrin's to reacting to irregularities in the road surface. Brakes are good, too, though the edge in this respect probably goes to the Darrin.

Corvette instruments, **left**, are spread out over the dash, while Darrin's, **below**, are conveniently grouped in front of driver. **Below center:** Both Corvette's and Darrin's tops go up and down more easily when two persons are on the job. Both tops stow neatly under permanently attached boots when down. **Bottom:** Darrin top may also be folded to landau or de ville position.

We confess to a prejudice against automatic transmissions in a car of this character — two-speed automatics especially! But putting aside our bias we must admit that the Powerglide does its job more effectively than we expected. The car's performance (see accompanying data page) speaks for itself.

Like the Darrin, the Corvette has a full set of gauges, including a tachometer and even a clock. So far, so good, but the placement of some of the instruments, low and far to the driver's right, makes them virtually impossible to read while the car is under way.

The Corvette's trunk is smaller than that of the Darrin, but still of usable dimensions. On the other hand, there are spacious storage compartments under the armrests on both doors. Like the Kaiser-Darrin, the Corvette has no storage compartment in the dash.

This was a fully restored car when Richard Carpenter bought it in Scottsdale, Arizona, some years ago. Nothing is known of its earlier history, nor is there any way of authenticating its 26,000-mile odometer reading. This 'Vette is a familiar sight to fans of The Carpenters, however, having appeared in one of Richard and Karen's TV specials a few years back.

Inevitably, of course, one comes down to the nitty-gritty question: Which to choose — the Kaiser-Darrin or the Chevrolet Corvette? As we reflected upon that one, we turned back in memory to the driveReport we did a few years ago on Steve LeFevre's 1953 Nash-Healey. In a sense, it's an unfair comparison, for the car cost some $1,500 more than either of the vehicles that are the subjects of this report. Yet the concept and the market target were essentially similar, so we can hardly ignore Donald Healey's multinational roadster.

And we have to say that in our view, price aside, the Nash-Healey takes it, hands down. It combines the performance of the Corvette with smoothness exceeding that of the Darrin. It is far more comfortable than either of them, and handles better as well. Whether the Nash-Healey's superiority is sufficient to justify the extra $1,500 may be open

What's in a Name?

Detroit discovered in the thirties what Ned Jordan had figured out years earlier: The name you give your car bears more than a little relationship to its market appeal!

By the fifties, evocative titles were the norm. Some — Newport, for instance — implied prestige. Others, like Roadmaster and Hornet, suggested performance. And so, you can bet that careful corporate consideration went into the selection of the monikers for our two comparisonReport cars.

In Navy jargon a Corvette is a small, fast, highly maneuverable vessel. What better name for this new breed of Chevrolet? Note that this was the first in a series of Chevrolet "C's" that appeared over the next few years: Corvair, Chevelle, Caprice, even Cameo in the division's truck line.

The selection of the Kaiser-Darrin's name, linking Kaiser to Howard Darrin's considerable prestige, reflects Henry Kaiser's (and Dutch Darrin's) shrewdness. By unanimous vote of a group of about 30 Kaiser executives, according to Darrin's later recollection, the car was to have been called the "DKF" — Darrin-Kaiser-Fraser. Dutch himself had suggested the hyphenated Kaiser-Darrin name, pointing out the potential confusion with the two-cycle German DKW automobile then being imported into the United States. When that unanimous vote came down it appeared that Darrin's suggestion was buried — until the Boss spoke up. With a broad smile Henry Kaiser quietly suggested, "I say we call it the Kaiser-Darrin."

And that was that!

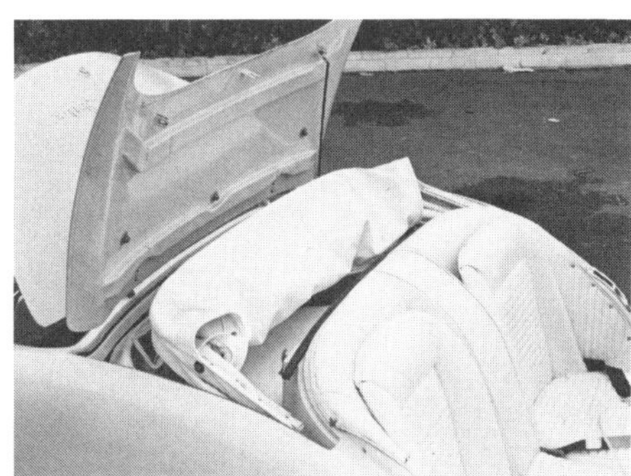

to question, however, and of course this evaluation does not apply to later Corvettes with their V-8 engines, four-speed transmissions and refined suspension systems.

All of which admittedly begs the question. We found the Kaiser-Darrin to be the more interesting of the two cars under consideration here, and by far the more attractive in its styling—the latter being a matter of taste, we realize. We prefer its stick-and-overdrive transmission to the Chevy Powerglide, the Kaiser's sloppy linkage notwithstanding. Overall, we'd take it over the Corvette— *if* it was to be used primarily for short-haul driving. But for sheer competence on the open road and in the mountains, and for long-distance travel with some acceptable measure of comfort, the nod would clearly have to go to the Corvette. Likewise, for plain dollar value the Corvette is the clear choice.

And if both these cars are in some respects a little crude, remember that auto makers on this side of the Atlantic were rather out of practice, in 1954, when in came to building sports cars. They would do better, as time went along! ◌

Acknowledgments and Bibliography

"*Here Come the Corvettes*," Popular Mechanics, *December 1953;* "*Desert Road Test: The Kaiser-Darrin 161*," Motor Life, *October 1954;* "*Kaiser Plastic Sports Car Goes Into Production*," Popular Mechanics, *March 1954;* "*Steel Company and Top Designer Collaborate on First Plastic Car*," Old Cars, *October 16-31, 1973;* Robert C. Ackerson, "*Kaiser-Darrin 161*," Old Cars, *November 7, 1978;* John R. Bond, "*The Chevrolet Corvette*," Road & Track, *June 1954;* Floyd Clymer, "*Clymer Road Tests the Corvette*," Popular Mechanics, *October 1954;* Spence Murray, Special Interest American Cars; *Wilbur Shaw,* "*Plastic Kaiser Shows Its Sporty Ways*," Popular Science, *August 1954;* Rich Taylor, "*The American Sports Car*," Old Cars, *November 2, 1976.*

Our thanks to Ralph Dunwoodie, Sun Valley, Nevada; Vince and Franca Manocchi, Azusa, California; John Parker, Fullerton, California; Telford and Ada Work, Pacific Palisades, California. Special thanks to Richard Carpenter, Santa Fe Springs, California; John Fawcett, La Jolla, California; Jim Ogle, Santa Fe Springs, California.

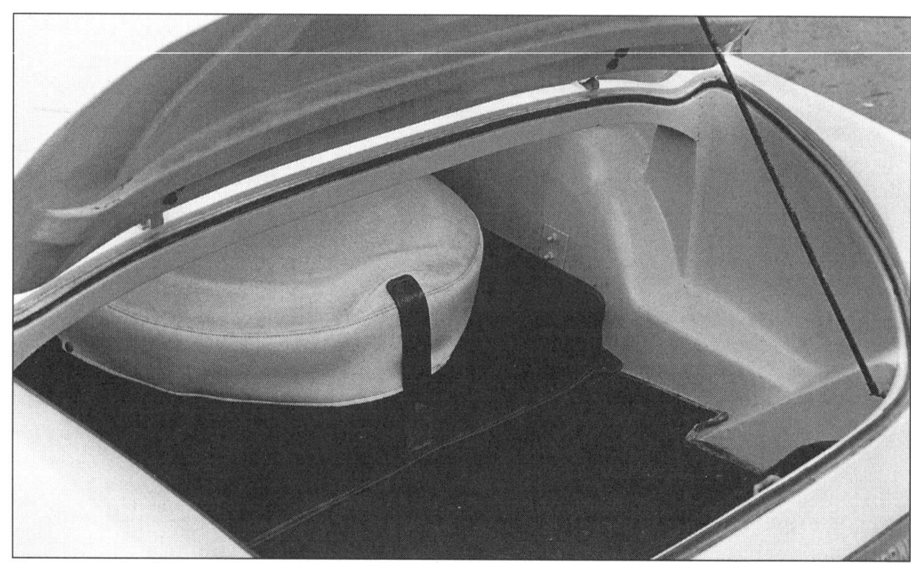

Corvette, below, wins the trunk space sweepstakes thanks to hiding its spare tire under the trunk floor.

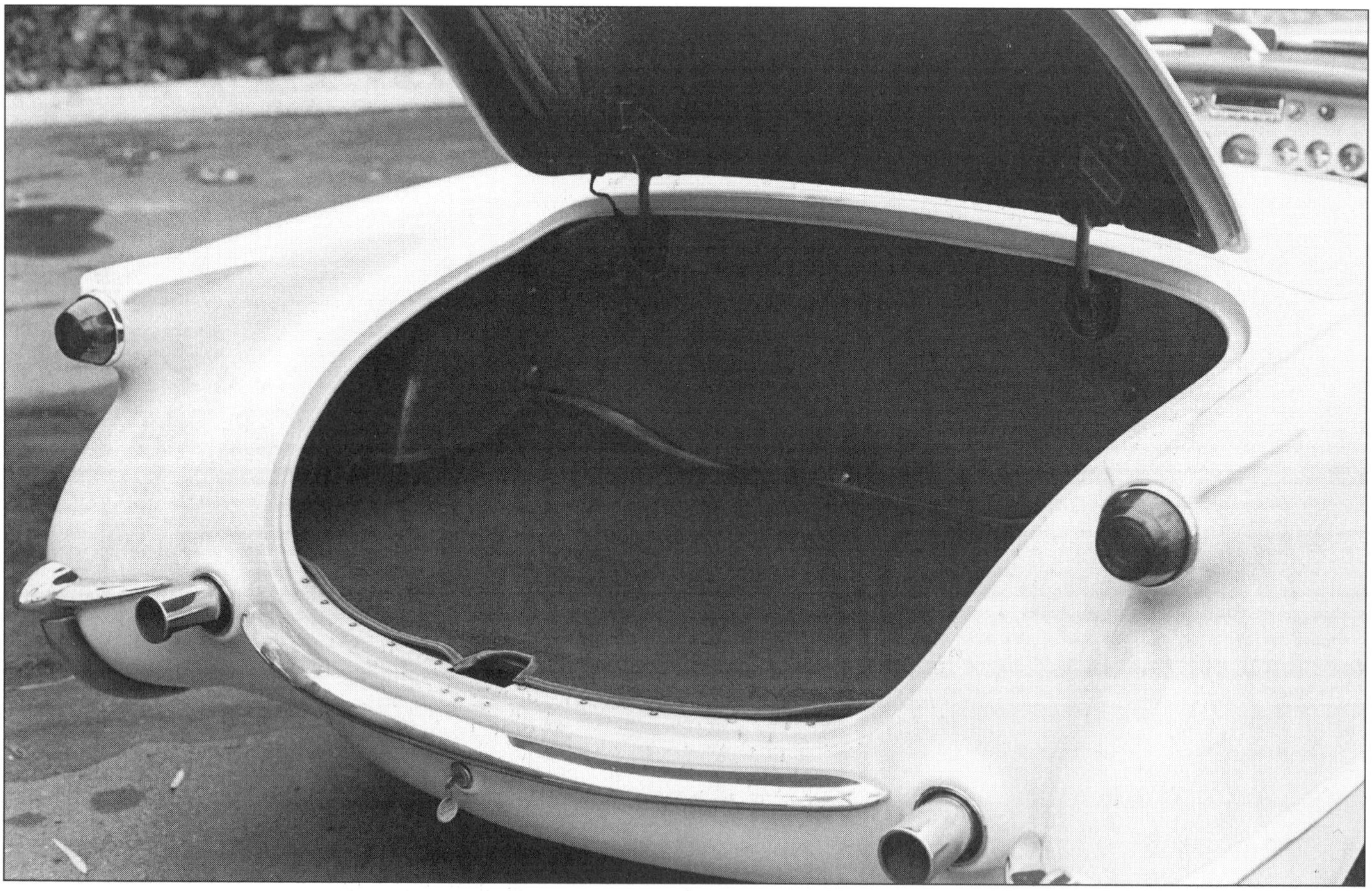

Now the most exciting new car for '54...!

Kaiser·Darrin 161

America's newest and finest sports car!

You've seen other new cars for '54, but nothing as exciting as this. It's the fabulous Kaiser-Darrin 161—the new name in sports cars, the last word in elegance— in production and for sale!

Its armour-clad Fiberglas body is the lowest, sleekest on the road. Its revolutionary sliding doors and disappearing Deauville-style top set a refreshing new fashion. Its elegance of appointment challenges custom designers either side of the Atlantic.

Styled by Darrin of Paris and built by the great new Kaiser-Willys combination, it has an amazingly high power-to-weight ratio that assures highest competitive performance.

Ask your Kaiser-Willys dealer about it today. (If he doesn't have it now, he'll have it soon!) And drive it—soon! It's the outstanding pleasure car of our time!

Another outstanding product of the great new Kaiser-Willys combination,

makers of the beautiful Kaiser   the smart Aero Willys

1955 CORVETTE

The First High-Performance 'Vette

by Tim Howley
photos by David Gooley

NINETEEN fifty-five is a bewildering and little-known Corvette year with a mere 700 units produced, Corvette's lowest production year next to 1953. Yet it is a highly significant year, marking the birth of the V-8 and the beginning of Corvette high performance. To understand the year you have to go back two years earlier to the Corvette's origins.

In the early fifties the European sports car invaded US shores. It was led by the MG-TD and Jaguar XK 120, followed by the Nash-Healey, Austin-Healey, Triumph TR, etc. A sports car market of an estimated 20,000 had grown up overnight, especially in Southern California. Now GM's styling czar, Harley Earl, was keenly aware of this. In fact he had a son entering college whose classmates were driving around in new XK Jags and MGs.

Earl began sketching a mid-sized GM sports car with a V-8 engine. What Earl envisioned was a $1,000 sports car for collegiates who couldn't afford Jags and MGs. He showed his simple sketches to Bob McLean, a recently hired designer-engineer. McLean in turn laid out several full-sized views with major components in place. His version had a six-cylinder engine. At this point it was all pretty academic. No one upstairs had ordered a GM sports car. But a number of other events at GM at the time would change things.

Two GM Motorama cars, the LeSabre and XP-300, were meeting with wide public approval. The sports car styling was already there, it just had to be reduced in size. Then came the 1953 Motorama and the need for a Chevrolet entry. Earl's little roadster caught the attention of Ed Cole who was then general manager of Chevrolet. Engineers assigned to the project included Bob McLean, Vince Kaptur

Originally published in Special Interest Autos #160, Jul.-Aug. 1997

Top left: Spinner-style wheel covers began with '53 Vette. *Left:* Crossed flags motif has also been a Corvette symbol since the fifties. *Above:* Front end is unchanged from earlier cars. *Below:* V-8 equipped cars have enlarged gold "v" as part of fender i.d.

Sr., Ed Cole and Maurice Olley. But even at this point there was no serious thought of putting the car into production.

The original idea was to build for show only America's answer to the Jaguar. In fact, the wheelbase was set at the same 102 inches. It was a two-seat roadster with simple and very American lines, and for the time a minimum of chrome. The cockpit sat just forward of the rear axle and the engine sat as low as a Chevrolet six could without scraping up pavement. The chassis was a rather conventional X type, but the body was the new miracle material, fiberglass, or as it was called then, Glass Reinforced Plastic or GRP.

The front suspension was taken directly from the 1949-54 Chevrolet passenger car, only the coil springs were a little heavier. The rear end was Hotchkiss driven with leaf springs located outboard of the chassis. The stove-bolt Chevrolet six was tweaked from 108 horsepower to 150 with a hot cam, higher compression ratio, three Carter YH carburetors mounted on the side to clear the hood, and dual exhausts. There were also solid valve lifters and dual-rate valve springs. Powerglide was the only transmission. A three-speed stick was never offered until very late in 1955. Later in the year horsepower was raised to 155.

The Corvette was the Chevrolet Division's contribution to the 1953 Motorama. It was the sensation of the show, and the widespread Motorama success was the main reason why the Corvette was immediately put into production. The next year two other cars accompanied the Corvette to the 1954 Motorama. They were the Nomad station wagon and Corvair fastback. Both of these cars were based on the same chassis as the Corvette and had similar fiberglass bodies. In the case of the Nomad, the wheelbase was stretched to 115 inches and the overall length to 191 inches. The Nomad was so well received that it later became offered as a version of the 1955 Chevrolet. The Corvair's fastback styling inspired the sixties Corvette Sting Ray.

Fiberglass was chosen for the body not only because it was then viewed as somewhat of an exotic space age material, but because the car could quickly be put in production in limited numbers. It would have taken much longer to gear up for Kirksite dies to stamp out steel bodies, and far more steel-bodied cars would have to be built just to break even.

The first Corvette rolled out of the factory in Flint, Michigan, the only place it was produced, in late September 1953. A lot has been written that it was not very successful at first. The truth was that Flint could only produce about five

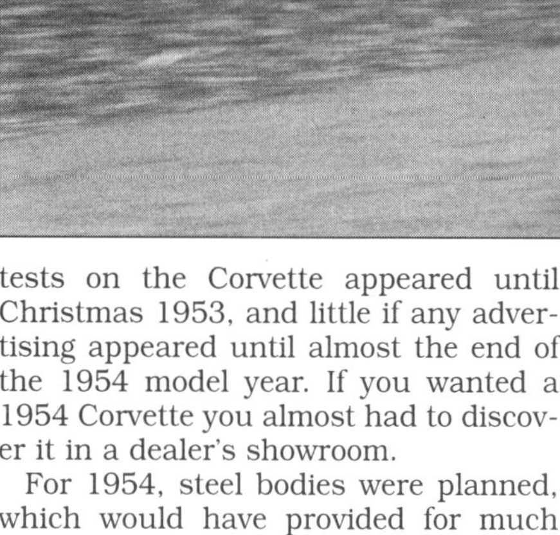

Above left: Mesh stone guards lend a competition-car aura. Above right: Taillamp treatment was carried over from '53 and '54. Below: Toothy grille is more dream car than sports car. Right: Dropping in new Chevy V-8 and upgrading its power for Corvette transformed the car to a high-performance contender.

1955 Corvette

a day in the earliest months, and most of these went to important figures in major corporations and important political and military figures. By the end of 1953 only 300 Corvettes had been produced.

All of the original 300 1953 Corvettes were identical, white with red interiors. The base price of $3,498 including Powerglide hardly reflected Earl's original intent, but it was still a lot less expensive than a Jaguar. The only extras were signal-seeking AM radio, heater and whitewall tires. All were sold with all these extras except perhaps whitesidewall tires.

The Corvette went into 1954 essentially unchanged. Production was moved to St. Louis, where 1,000 cars a month could be built. Originally Chevrolet thought they could sell 10,000 1954 models. By now it was evident that sales would not meet expectations: 3,640 were built by model year end, but only about 2,500 had been sold. It would be 1956 before the Corvette would begin to sell in any numbers.

Quite a number of reasons have been cited for the poor sales performance of the 1954 Corvette. Originally it was planned to sell a lot of them to celebrities. The celebrities did not buy them in the numbers anticipated. There was at the time a widespread misunderstanding as to what constituted a sports car. While it certainly was a true sports car, many purists did not view it as such. As a sports car, the Corvette did not have roll-down side windows or a hardtop that could be attached. Consequently, it leaked to an annoying degree. The six-cylinder engine, lack of a manual transmission and a degree of handling problems have also been attributed to the 1954 Corvette's limited sales.

But the overriding reason may have been lack of advertising and publicity. The division at the time simply was not geared to promoting the car. It was sort of a situation of, well now we have it, so what are we going to do with it? No road tests on the Corvette appeared until Christmas 1953, and little if any advertising appeared until almost the end of the 1954 model year. If you wanted a 1954 Corvette you almost had to discover it in a dealer's showroom.

For 1954, steel bodies were planned, which would have provided for much higher production. But fiberglass bodies were continued, which at the time did not permit very high production.

1955 saw the introduction of Chevrolet's new 265-c.i.d. ohv V-8. The manual transmission was not available until very late in the year, and even then only an estimated 75 or so were so equipped, none of them sixes.

The V-8 engine offered in 1955 was technically not an option. The engine was a modification of the 265-c.i.d. Chevrolet passenger car engine introduced that same year. With its 195-horsepower rating, as opposed to 162 horsepower for the standard engine, it is similar but not identical to the 1955 Chevrolet with power-pak. It has a revised cam and solid lifters, but the compression ratio remains at 8.0:1. It is

equipped with a four-barrel carburetor, automatic choke, and longer mufflers than previous six-cylinder models. V-8 ignition shielding consists of chrome distributor and coil covers with bails, braided and grounded plug wires, and wire carriers behind the exhaust manifolds. Valve covers of the 1955 V-8 models are chrome plated with Chevrolet scripts. The 1955 Corvette did not share the 1955 Chevrolet's new ball joint front suspension. The old 1949-54 Chevrolet front suspension was retained through 1962.

There were some modifications made at the front of the frame to accommodate the V-8 engine. There were some very minor cockpit modifications. For example the manual choke space is blank on the instrument panel.

The V identification, a large gold V on the side, separates the eight from the six for identification purposes. Otherwise the models are identical in styling and detail. Six-cylinder models are virtual duplicates of the 1954 models and still have the six-volt electrical system. It is unclear how many six-cylinder models were produced for 1955, probably no more than a dozen.

For 1955 there was a choice of a Polo White, Harvest Gold, Gypsy Red, Corvette Copper and Pennant Blue. 1955 is the most confusing of all model years regarding color. Just how many colors were factory applied remains a mystery. Also not clear are soft top colors and materials. Earlier models have a canvas top. Sometime during 1955 vinyl tops appeared.

Corvettes did not have power steering and power brakes until 1963, and the 1955 list of options was as basic as James Dean's wardrobe. The complete list was simply directional lights, $16.75; heater, $91.40; signal-seeking radio, $145,15; Powerglide, $178; windshield washer, $11.85; parking brake alarm, $5.65; courtesy lights, $4.05; and whitewall tires, $26.90. Except for radio, heater, and whitewall tires, the complete list was mandatory.

Some were sold new with blackwall tires, but only one has been found without a heater. $2,774 was the base price for a six, $2,909 was the base price for the eight. With either engine you paid extra for the Powerglide. If you ordered the six you got a 155-horsepower "Tri carb" engine. With the V-8 you got a 195-horsepower engine with four-barrel carburetor.

Hardtops were not available through 1955, but aftermarket hardtops were marketed by some dealers.

With the smashing success of the 1955 Chevrolet passenger car and the introduction of the V-8 on the Corvette, many will ask why only 700 Corvettes were built for the 1955 model year, making this Corvette's lowest year of production except 1953. The reasons are many and still do not provide a complete answer.

With over 1,000 unsold 1954 Corvettes on hand at the beginning of the 1955 model year, Chevrolet was slow to produce the 1955 models. In an article on early Chevrolet V-8 performance in *Special Interest Autos* #27, March-April, 1975, Karl Ludvigsen wrote, "The art of creating hybrid engine/car combinations was still in its infancy, and anyway Chevy had first to meet the demand for

specifications

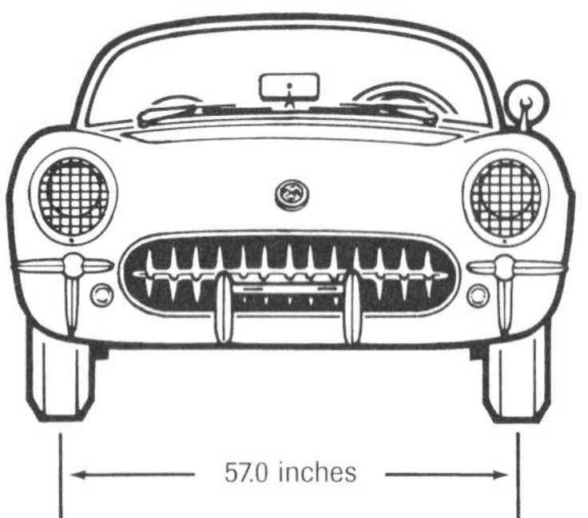

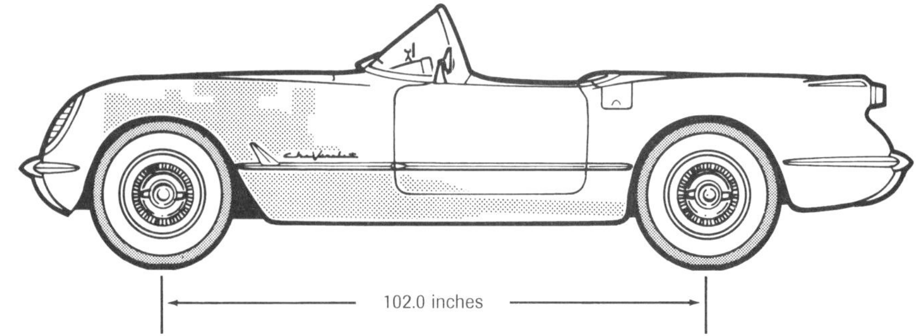

1955 Corvette two-passenger roadster

Base price	$2,909
Price as equipped	$3,389
Options	Carries all the mandatory options which are directional lights, windshield wipers, parking brake alarm light, courtesy lights, plus the non-mandatory options of signal-seeking radio, heater, and whitewall tires

ENGINE

Type	Ohv V-8
Bore x stroke	3.75 inches x 3 inches
Displacement	265 cubic inches
Compression ratio	8.0:1
Horsepower @ rpm	195 @ 5,000
Torque @ rpm	N/A
Valve lifters	Hydraulic
Main bearings	5
Induction system	Carter 4-bbl
Fuel system	Vacuum pump, camshaft driven
Exhaust system	Dual

TRANSMISSION

Type	Powerglide 2-speed automatic with torque converter
Ratios: 1st	2.1:1
2nd	1.82:1
3rd	1.00:1
Reverse	1.82:1

DIFFERENTIAL

Type	Hotchkiss, spiral bevel gears
Ratio	3.55:1
Drive axles	Semi-floating

STEERING

Type	Semi-irreversible worm and sector
Turns lock-to-lock	4.5
Ratio	16:1
Turn circle	36.75 feet

BRAKES

Type	4-wheel drums, hydraulic, internal expanding
Drum diameter	11 inches
Effective area	154.4 square inches

CHASSIS & BODY

Frame	Box-girder steel, X-member double dropped
Body	Laminated fiberglass-reinforced plastic
Body style	2-door, 2-passenger roadster, manual top, side curtains

SUSPENSION

Front	Independent, unequal A-arms, coil springs, stabilizer bar, tubular hydraulic shock absorbers
Rear	Longitudinal leaf springs, hydraulic shock absorbers
Tires	6.70 x 15 4-ply tube type
Wheels	Drop-center rim, pressed steel

WEIGHTS AND MEASURES

Wheelbase	102.0 inches
Overall length	167.0 inches
Overall width	72.24 inches
Overall height	51.25 inches
Front track	57.0 inches
Rear track	59.0 inches
Ground clearance	6.0 inches
Shipping weight	2,750 pounds

CAPACITIES

Crankcase	5 quarts
Cooling system	17.75
Fuel tank	17.25 gallons

*Far left: Round plastic knobs serve as inside and outside door handles. **Above left:** driveReport car is 385th 1955 Corvette built. **Below left:** Symmetrical instrument layout makes oil and amp gauges difficult for driver to see. **Facing page:** Chromed valve covers distinguish Corvette engine from Chevy passenger car V-8s.*

1955 Corvette

the new engines from its own customers in that boom sales year of 1955. In fact, that's the reason why the Corvette, such an obvious choice to be given V-8 power, didn't get the new engine as an option until mid-way through the 1955 model year. Chevy wanted to keep the V-8 for the sedans, and use the Corvette to keep attention focused on the old Blue Flame Six. It was just the opposite approach from what enthusiasts expected."

According to Bert Lukins, a 1955 authority in the National Corvette Restorers Society, Ludsvigsen's statement is not completely accurate. The 1955 Chevrolet came as a V-8 from the beginning of its production in January 1955 through January 1956 when the 1956 Corvette began production.

Another factor in the 1955 Corvette's limited production was that Ford introduced its Thunderbird for 1955. While not exactly a sports car, its all steel body, roll up windows, optional hardtop and more conventional styling gave it far wider appeal than the Corvette. Ford produced 16,155 Thunderbirds for the 1955 model year. Chevrolet's feeling, at least for the time being, was why even bother to compete. A further deterrent to 1955 Corvette sales was lack of a standard transmission for the V-8 until

the very end of the model year.

However the underlying reason had to be that the Chevrolet Division simply did not choose to build more than 700 Corvettes.

During this period, Zora Arkus-Duntov rescued the Corvette from certain extinction and made the 1956 model the first true racing Corvette. Still, production that year was only 3,467. 1957 production was up to 6,339. In 1958, a sharp recession year, production was up to 9,168. Still it would be 1966 before Corvette production would equal and top that of the 1955 Thunderbird.

Driving Impressions

Our '55 Corvette driveReport car is owned by Jim Haight, founder of Bonanza Corvettes in San Diego. The business sells vintage and used Corvettes, and has about 100 in stock at all times. Corvettes like this one are the personal property of the founder, not for sale at any price. Moreover, this one is an all-original car with 91,000 miles, and is

The Corvette, Nomad and Corvair

The 1953-55 Corvette had very strong ties with the Nomad dream car introduced at the 1954 GM Motorama. The Nomad had the same grille/front clip as the Corvette tied to a Nomad station wagon body. It was a fiberglass job constructed on the Corvette chassis and was 191 inches overall compared to the Corvette's length of 167 inches. The wheelbase was stretched from 102 to 115 inches. The height, at 54 inches, was one inch higher than the height of the Corvette and the width, at 71 inches, was about one inch wider than that of the Corvette. It had a Chevrolet Blue Flame six-cylinder engine developing 150 horsepower, same as the Corvette and 25 horsepower more than the standard 1954 Chevrolet with Powerglide. The production 1955 Nomad was inspired by this show car, but it was built on a standard 1955 Chevrolet chassis.

Accompanying the Corvette and the

Nomad at the 1954 Motorama was the Corvair. This car also had a Corvette body, a 102-inch Corvette chassis and 150-horsepower, six-cylinder Corvette engine. The difference was that this car was an enclosed fastback. Except for a height of 51 inches, the measurements and specifications were the same as the 1954 Corvette. Three air intakes at the sides of the front fenders were functional and unique to the Corvair. These vents supplied air to the passenger compartment, not the engine. Just behind the rear quarter windows were three air exhaust vents. This ducting system was controlled by manual buttons inside the car. A recessed area at the trailing edge of the fastback housed the license plate and backup lights which were mounted on a bright metal plate embossed with small Chevrolet emblems. Engine compartment ventilators were mounted at each side of the hood.

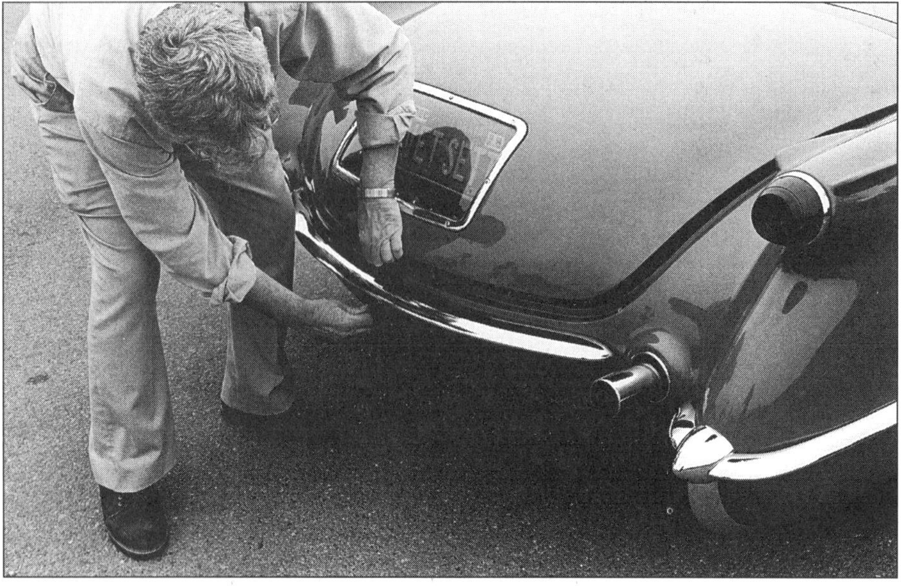

1955 Corvette

signed under the hood by Zora Arkus-Duntov, a key member of the original Corvette team and Corvette chief engineer in 1956.

Jim Haight bought the car 15 years ago from a friend who was going through a divorce. He believes it to be the finest all-original 1955 Corvette in existence. The serial number of this one is E55S001385, meaning it was the 385th of 700 built.

While any '55 Corvette looks as sporty as Rock Hudson, and most have the V-8 engine, underneath all are about as exciting as Mr. Peepers. Within this Motorama dream car lurked Aunt Maude's Chevrolet sedan, shortened, tuned, fit-

*Top: Despite the much better performance offered by the V-8, the '55 Corvette was a slow seller, with only 700 examples produced. **Above:** Trunk release is hidden below bumper. **Below:** Prominent stitching makes doors look more kustom kar than sports car.*

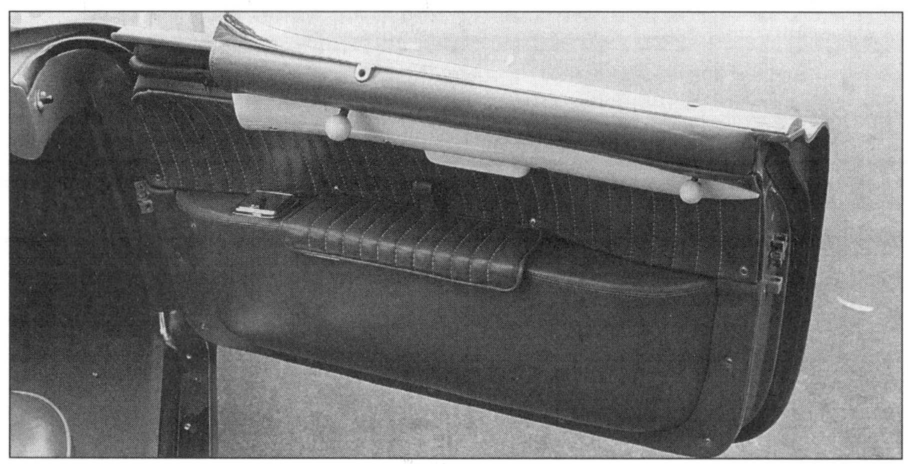

How Many Are Left?

According to Bert Lukins, 1955 Corvette authority within the National Corvette Restorers Society, of the 700 built, as many as 350 may be left. That is an extremely high survival rate for any car. For the 1955 Corvette there are quite a number of reasons. It was a rare car when it was one year old and owners knew it. All Corvettes are collectible, and the early ones have been especially cherished for a long, long time. Moreover Corvettes have the benefit of a fiberglass body which does not rust out.

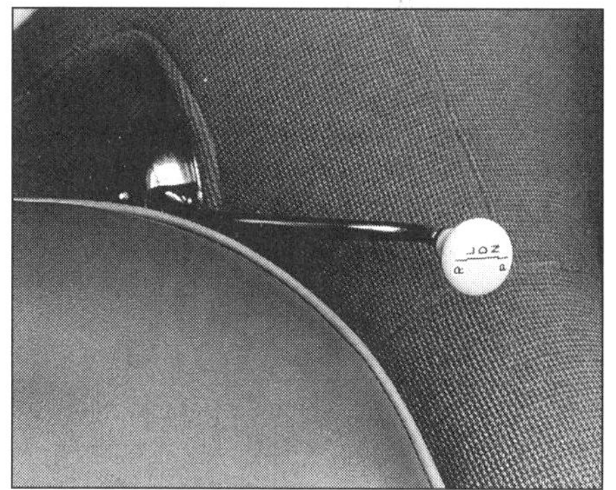

Above: *There's a surfeit of chrome on and around the dash.* ***Below:*** *Baffling Power-glide control comes out of side of tunnel like early Austin-Healey shifters.* ***Right:*** *Windshield and cockpit design give a cozy, intimate feel to interior.*

ted with an open drive line and Hotchkiss rear suspension, and, horror of horrors, a two-speed Powerglide.

In retrospect, the chassis specifications look pathetic for a high-performance sports car. However, you must judge the model in mid-fifties perspective, before Duntov got hold of it. While the car appears klutzy in comparison to Corvettes since, it compared quite favorably in performance and handling with other sports cars of its day. A '55 Corvette could sprint from 0-60 in under 9 seconds and easily achieve 100 mph.

Chevrolet made no bones that the Corvette was built to compete with the Jaguar XKs. Unfortunately this resulted in poor driver-to-wheel position, mediocre handling, and dicey brakes. Had Ferrari, Maserati, Alfa Romeo, Mercedes-Benz or Porsche been the target, the Corvette might have had a happier beginning.

From its inception, the early Corvette was a compromise. Springs were soft front and rear. Suspension and a large diameter roll bar produced an annoying amount of understeer. Maurice Olley's suspension system placed the rear leaf springs far outboard and angled them inward from their fronts to ensure lots of roll understeer. Front suspension remained stock Chevrolet with only a stabilizer bar added.

We felt that the '55 Corvette gave a firm, smooth ride, and although hardly thrilling in the turns, was quite safe and forgiving. In fact, we were surprised at the rather small amount of lean. Overall, however, we had to rate it as a

"boulevard" car as apposed to the XK-120 with its stiffer ride and true sports car cornering capabilities. Looking back, we will be first to admit that in the 1955 road races where Corvette did compete, it fared quite nicely.

Among our minor petty peeves, the shifting arrangement left us totally confused. The automatic floor shift is reverse, then low, drive, neutral and park in an odd zig-zag pattern. Windshield washer is actuated by the floor pedal. Opening the doors is even more confusing. The forward knob is to open the door and the backward knob is a release control for the side curtains. Of course, there are no outside door handles. You will never get into the trunk until you finally discover that the unlock button is concealed underneath the trunklid. On the plus side we liked the simple, straightforward arrangement of the instruments which are, left to right: fuel,

Bonanza Corvettes Rooted in a San Diego Family Business Started in 1910

Bonanza Corvettes is a San Diego, California, institution that traces its history back to early in the century when grandfather Lloyd Haight opened a Cadillac and Oldsmobile dealership at the corner of East Broadway and 16th in 1910, kitty-corner from where Bonanza Corvettes stands today.

His son Jim joined his father's business in the late thirties. At age 18 Jim joined the Air Corps. After World War II Lloyd Haight sold out the agency which was then selling Oldsmobiles. In 1946 Jim went to work as a salesman for the new owner, soon rising to sales manager, becoming the youngest sales manager in the United States. In 1953 Jim opened his own used car lot.

"When the Corvettes came out in '53, I decided that San Diego needed somebody who would really push these Corvettes," recalls Jim Haight. "So I started handling [used] Corvettes, and I have ever since, and it has treated me very well."

The present Bonanza Corvette building is across the street from grandfather Lloyd's dealership. In about 1937 Lloyd Haight acquired this property and facility and gave it to his son, Jim, who for many years leased it to Chevrolet dealers, then to a community college as a technical training center. In about 1975, Jim Haight and his son Glenn opened Bonanza Corvettes at another location. In about 1980 the Bo-nanza Corvettes business was moved to its present location and Jim Haight still owns the building after 60 years.

The success of the business today is based primarily on word of mouth and the Haight family's many years in the automobile business. It is now managed by Jim's son, Glenn, although Dad remains active in the business.

Son Glenn says, "We buy most of our cars at curbside. People know that we are in the business, and we are offered cars before other people know they are for sale. Occasionally we buy cars at auction, but mostly we buy cars from private parties. A lot of the cars are cars that we have sold before. Since we offer financing, we establish relationships where people are coming in every month."

Bonanza Corvettes can well boast being the very last of the East Broadway, San Diego, dealerships. This area was once a major auto dealer row in the city. A few of the lots still remain, now vacant, or occupied by the San Diego homeless or auto body shops. A fine art deco Ford dealership from the thirties still stands at the corner of 12th and Broadway. It is now a wig shop. The other old-time San Diego auto dealer center, located at the west end of Broadway and extending to the north, has now been completely razed for the development of San Diego's Columbia high rise office buildings.

1955 Corvette

temperature, tachometer, then battery, oil pressure and finally a clock.

In an attempt to keep the car as low priced as possible, and a true sports car, there were side curtains instead of roll-up windows, no outside door handles, a fabric top only, no hardtop offered by the factory. There was a minimum of frills. Of course, all of this turned off the typical Chevrolet buyer, which was reflected in disappointing 1955 sales. ๏๏

*Top: driveReport car has been personally autographed by its chief creator. **Above:** Top can be completely concealed under fiberglass boot. **Below:** Side curtains have a tidy storage pouch in the trunk.*

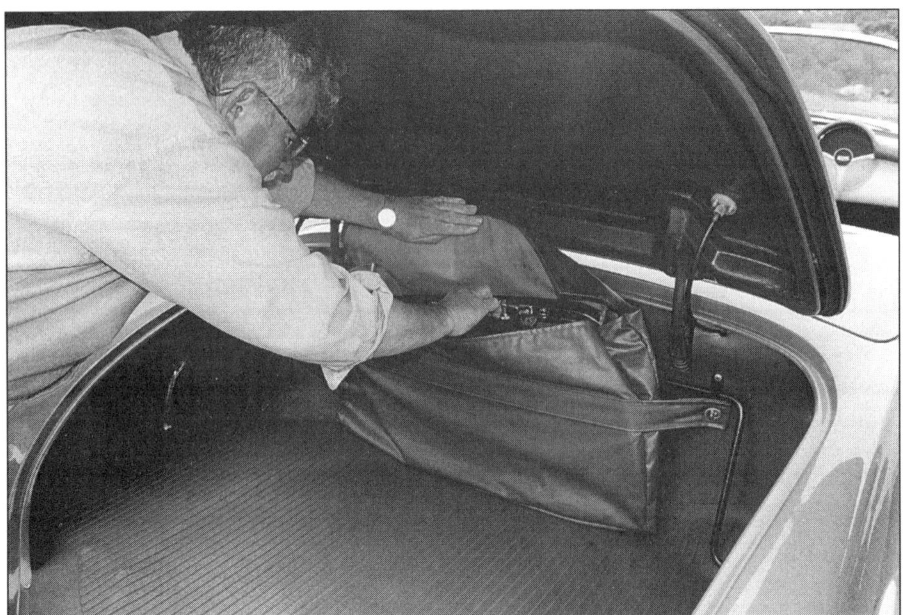

Acknowledgments and Bibliography

1954 Corvette driveReport, Special Interest Autos #3, Jan.-Feb. 1971; *GM's Motoramas*, SIA #21, March-April, 1974; "Clean Slate Car," "They Came to Us: '55 Chevy Racers," "Small-Blocks in Fast Wrappers: V-8 Chevy road racers," "Small Blocks in Fancy Wrappers: V-8 Chevy Gran Turismos," SIA # 27, March-April, 1975; "1955 Chevrolet Bel-Air V-8," SIA #123, June, 1991; "Corvettes, 1954-1968," Car Life, November, 1967; Standard Catalog of Chevrolet, 1912-1990, *Krause Publications*; NCRS, 1953-63 Corvette; The Corvette Black Book, *Motorbooks International*.

Special thanks to the Haight family of Bonanza Corvettes, San Diego, California, and Bert Lukins, Portland, Oregon, National Corvette Restorers Society.

Drive Reports

You will not find any drive reports on the 1955 Corvette in *Motor Trend*. Tom McCahill never tested one for *Mechanix Illustrated*. Supposedly, the only drive report ever done on the car was for *Road & Track* in 1955. Unfortunately, we have not been able to confirm or find that article.

Own a Corvette now!

It packs more sheer fun into every mile than any car you've ever driven!

Here's the car for fun . . . a swift-looking low-slung beauty that stands only 33 inches at door top, extends a compact 167 inches in length, and packs into a rugged sports-car chassis all the responsive power of a special 150-horsepower "Blue-Flame" engine with triple sidedraft carburetion. And now you can enjoy the thrill of owning a Corvette. It's on display by Chevrolet dealers—the same dealers who make Corvette parts and service available wherever you go. See your dealer and place your order now. . . . Chevrolet Division of General Motors, Detroit 2, Michigan.

First of the dream cars to come true 

CORVETTE SS
THE ONE AND ONLY!

by Rich Taylor
photos by Russell von Sauers

IN May of 1956, Harley Earl borrowed Jack Ensley's D-type Jaguar that had finished third at Sebring six weeks earlier. The General Motors vice-president of Styling then presented the car to his most advanced styling groups — known as the Research Studio and Studio Z — and told them to restyle it to look more like a Corvette, replace the tired-out Jaguar Six with a Corvette V-8 and convert the car to left-hand drive. Their deadline was The Twelve Hours of Sebring in March 1957.

Earl was a master of corporate games-manship. He thought that General Motors should be involved in international endurance racing, and the factory team had just proved at Sebring that the production Corvette was too heavy to compete with out-and-out sports/racers like the D-type Jag, Maserati 300S or Aston Martin DBR/1. But the only person at General Motors with the background and knowledge to create the necessary purpose-built racer was Zora Arkus-Duntov, who jealously guarded his own Corvette Engineering fiefdom...and had an extremely prickly personality.

At Sebring, Duntov had petulantly refused to have anything to do with the four-car Corvette team captained by former Mercedes team driver John Fitch, with the inevitable result that, as Fitch wryly put it, "We finished not as well as we had hoped, but better than we deserved." Fitch was on retainer to Chevrolet's advertising agency, Campbell-Ewald, as a "competition advisor." This meant, among other things, that he had virtually no horsepower to make things happen inside Corvette Engineering. Any racing program had to include Zora in order to succeed.

Fitch encouraged Harley Earl to get something going for 1957. Rather than directly ask Zora to get involved, which he would surely refuse, Earl constructed this elaborate ruse with Ensley's Jaguar, which of course he had no intention of pursuing. Duntov rose to the bait. In June of 1956, he and Harold Krieger were ordered by Chevrolet Engineering director Harry Barr to start fitting a V-8 to the Jaguar chassis.

Instead, Duntov sketched a rough outline for a world-class sports/racer, along with a written proposal for a four-car racing team to be entered at Sebring and LeMans. As he put it in his proposal, "Putting our engine in the Jaguar is like admitting that we are not capable of designing the whole car ourselves."

Ed Cole, who was then General Man-ager of Chevrolet and Duntov's ultimate boss, had been trying to get Zora involved in the Sebring racing program for over a year. He accepted the proposal immediately. Though neither of them ever mentioned it, it could easily have been Cole who put Earl up to the Jaguar ploy in the first place. The D-type was retained as a target car throughout the project. It was finally returned to Ensley in time for it to be repaired and brought to Sebring, where it retired. Ultimately, the car actually *was* fitted with a Corvette V-8 by racing mechanic Joe Silnes.

In July, well-known GM stylist Clare MacKichan was put in charge of what was now called Chevrolet Styling Experimental Project Number 64...XP-64 for short. Earl's heir apparent, Bill Mitchell, was also heavily involved, according to John Fitch. Within a few weeks, MacKichan's group had full-size renderings of XP-64, showing a Corvette toothed grille, twin hood "gunsights" and vertical quad driving lights in the fenders that could be aimed for cornering.

The original drawings show a single cockpit with stylized headrest cum tail-fin like Ensley's Jaguar and curious quad outside exhausts recessed into the Corvette's trademark cove panel, somewhat like the twin side exhausts of the Mercedes 300SLR. Over the next two months, this overly fussy stylist's

Originally published in Special Interest Autos #107, Sept.-Oct. 1988

*Above: SS styling is ultra-aggressive in appearance. **Left:** Headlamp treatment is like contemporary Ferrari and Maserati sports racers. **Below left:** Simple clips keep forward-hinged hood in place. **Below right:** Taillamps look like they were nipped from stock '58 Chevy.*

idea of what a race car should look like was pared down into the car which eventually appeared at Sebring. It was also given a new name...Corvette SS.

The final version still had the Corvette shark teeth grille, gunsights, and vented hood. Of all the features on the SS, drawing air in the grille opening and exhausting it through slots in the hood — *and flowing it across an interior aerodynamic surface to provide downforce* — was one of the cleverest. This could be the first use of such an aerodynamic device on any racing car, predating Ferrari's installation of a rear spoiler by six years, and the first use of front spoilers by nearly a decade. Ford's GT-40s were the next cars to use a similar underhood device.

The trick driving lights were replaced with single headlamps under plexiglass covers. A fixed accessory driving light was molded in beneath each headlamp, angled off to the side for cornering at night. The exhaust pipes got buried in the rocker panels, and the cove became a flush magnesium panel, horizontally striated like the rear fender trim on a '57 Chevy Bel Air. The distinctive pedestal-mounted headrest stayed, though without the tailfin. The cut-down plexiglass windscreen was now full-width, wrapping around onto the doors. Six round taillamps ranged across the functional rear grille, used for brake cooling.

Unlike every other Corvette ever built, the new car was not given a fiberglass body. And unlike most racing cars of that time, it wasn't aluminum, either. The master craftsmen in the prototype shop hand-hammered the entire thing out of sheet magnesium, with one-piece swing-up front and rear body sections.

The only other racing car with a similar body was the Mercedes-Benz 300SLR...it was the kind of extravagant gesture that only a Daimler-Benz or General Motors would attempt.

Magnesium is lightweight, but also fantastically expensive, flimsy and difficult to work with. But the reason other racing manufacturers didn't use it was that, unlike aluminum, magnesium burns with an almost explosive ferocity. When John Fitch's teammate Pierre Levegh plowed into the crowd at LeMans in 1955, killing over 90 spectators, it was flaming bits of magnesium bodywork that produced much of the carnage. Looking back, it is almost inconceivable that GM could have built a magnesium-bodied car, less than 18 months after that fateful LeMans.

Compared to other racing cars, except perhaps for the Mercedes factory team, the SS was immaculately finished to show car standards. Bill Mitchell had it painted in his favorite Marina Blue Metallic, with white roundels for the numbers...American racing colors. The interior was completely finished off in matching blue vinyl. There were two

form-fitting bucket seats, so corporate guests could be taken for rides. The dash was given a full set of white on black instruments in brushed aluminum housings, and the chrome shift lever was given a cast alloy shift knob. The three-spoke, mahogany-rim steering wheel was made quick-detach, like those in Mercedes racing cars.

At the same time the stylists were refining their ideas, Zora Arkus-Duntov started work on a chassis to fit under this elaborate bodywork. He built himself a drafting room right in the corner of the Chevrolet Engineering prototype shop, where drawings, a prototype chassis and individual components could be created side-by-side. The basic parameters of size and proportion had been determined by Duntov's original June proposal, but many of the engineering details were dictated by the shape of Styling's bodywork.

The actual written work orders to build four racing cars for Sebring weren't sent out until September. One car was to be completed in time for the New York Auto Show in December, where the Sebring attempt would be announced to

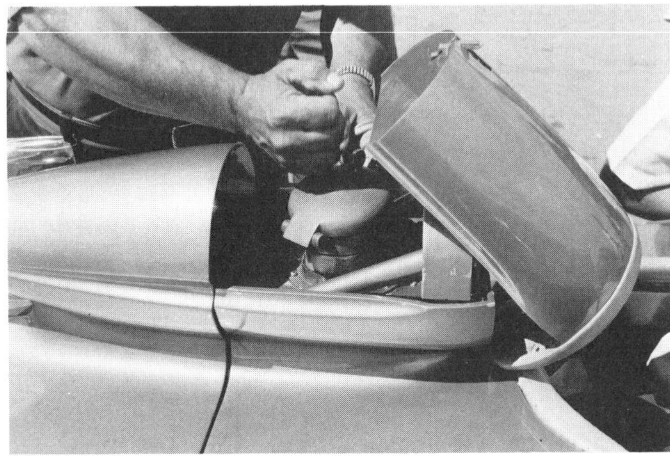

Above left: John Fitch gets ready for a few hot laps at Laguna Seca. Above right: Huge fuel filler cap hides in headrest. Below left: Exhaust pipes exit neatly before rear wheel arches. Below center and right: There are plenty of air vents in the hood.

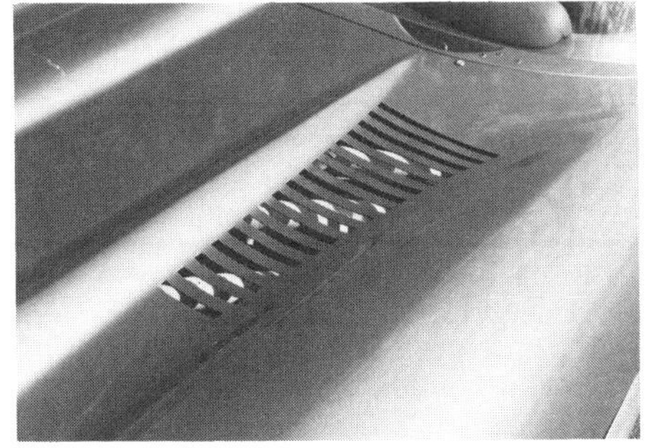

CORVETTE SS

the public, while the other three were to be finished in time for the race in March. In October, the SS program was cut to a single-car entry for Sebring, with the possibility of additional funding for LeMans if the car showed promise. The December date was now dismissed as unrealistic. Even with the GM resources that Zora Duntov had at his disposal, creating a race car from scratch takes more than six weeks.

Time and money were so short, that John Fitch says Zora "just took a Mercedes-Benz 300SL chassis and copied it." Certainly, the "birdcage" space frame built of small tubes looks very similar. The Mercedes 300SL had a 94.5-inch wheelbase, the D-type Jaguar 90.0 inches, the Maserati 300S 91.0 inches, the Ferrari 250 Testa Rossa 92.5 inches. The 92.0-inch wheelbase of the Corvette SS was thus right in line with its competition at the time.

To save time, Duntov used as many standard parts as possible, starting with a Rochester fuel-injected, 283-cubic-inch Corvette V-8. A special intake manifold was cast up with straight ram pipes and an air intake in the SS hood, but wind tunnel tests proved that air wasn't flowing to the intake. At Sebring, the car used a standard Corvette manifold fed by a fiberglass duct from the grille which was claimed to add 10 horsepower at high speeds.

Special 9.0:1 compression ratio aluminum heads and a deep-sump magnesium oil pan were made up, along with elaborately curving, 40-inch-long, individual exhaust headers. These headers had to route up and over the top of the space frame, then down to exit into a single large-diameter collector under the doors. Of course, the V-8 used the new low-lift, wide-overlap "Duntov" solid-lifter cam which Zora had developed for the 150-mph "production" Corvette he brought to Daytona Speed Weeks in February of 1956.

Output of the SS engine was given as 310 horsepower at 6,000 rpm, 295 lb-ft of torque at 4,400 rpm. This was roughly comparable to the power output of the Maseratis, Ferraris and Jaguars with which the SS was designed to compete. Redline was 7,000 rpm, but the drivers were advised to shift at 6,400 during the race itself, with a maximum limit of 6,800 rpm.

Duntov had an aluminum clutch housing cast up for the special heavy-duty clutch, along with an aluminum case for the four-speed Borg-Warner transmission...the first of the aluminum-case four-speeds which later became standard equipment on Chevrolet high-performance cars of all sorts right up until the present day. A set of special close-ratio gears was fitted, with ratios of 1.87, 1.54, 1.22 and direct drive in fourth.

The differential was an off-the-shelf Halibrand quick-change. Surprisingly, it was not fitted with a Positraction differential, even though limited-slip was already *de rigueur* on road racers, even 30 years ago. Equally surprisingly, Duntov's men made their own gearsets rather than use the wide selection of available Halibrand gears. Some sources say the car ran at Sebring with a 3.55:1 ratio, others say 3.87:1. Perhaps both were tried in practice, says John Fitch. Top speed: roughly 143 to 156 mph with a 7,000 rpm redline, depending on gearing. For LeMans, a 2.80:1 final drive would have been installed, good for a top speed of 180 mph.

The Halibrand quick-change was bolted solidly to a mounting plate in the birdcage. A large DeDion tube made from three-inch diameter tubing curved from the fabricated hub carriers around the back of the differential. Duntov added two trailing arms on each side, angled to provide lateral location for the wheels. There was no rear anti-roll bar. In 1956, this was a very conventional racing rear suspension, similar in design to those used on everything from the Lotus Eleven to the Ferrari Testa Rossa.

The front suspension consisted of simple parallel upper and lower A-arms, hand-built from sheet steel, with an anti-roll bar. They look like miniature versions of stock mid-fifties Chevrolet suspension pieces, though in actual fact they are completely different. Suspension was by coil-over shock-absorber/spring units. At the front they nest

inside the A-arms; at the rear, they angle inward to high fabricated mounting points tied together with a hefty tubular crossmember. Duntov's sole innovation was the use of "rising rate" springs which get progressively stiffer as they are compressed. The Corvette SS was one of the first cars built with what is now a standard practice on cars of all types.

In the fall of 1956, disc brakes were still a rare and relatively unknown quantity, even on front-rank racing cars. Among the leaders, only Jaguar, Aston Martin and Lotus used discs, and many drivers complained about the lack of "feel" compared to self-energizing drum brakes. The non-power boosted disc brake systems of that era also required tremendous pedal effort, which made the cars extremely fatiguing to drive in endurance races.

At the time, the most advanced drum brakes available were Chrysler Center-Plane units. These had drums 12 inches in diameter and 2.5 inches wide. The Chrysler brakes were made using the famous Al-Fin method, in which aluminum cooling fins were bonded to a cast-iron drum. Duntov modified them by drilling 120 small holes in the drum, so that when the aluminum fins were added, the aluminum flowed right into the braking surface through these holes. This gave even better heat transfer than the Chrysler design.

The famous Carl Kiekhaefer Chrysler AAA stock cars used these brakes on two-ton Chrysler 300s, and Briggs Cunningham had been using them for years on his Cunningham endurance racers, so they were already a well-proven commodity. Duntov's modified version of these same brakes later appeared in production on the 1957 Buick Model 75, and became a Buick trademark for years. Buick brakes were very popular with American race car builders until the mid-sixties, and the Bocars, Cheetahs and Old Yellers used them, among others.

Zora mounted the front brakes inside 5 x 15 inch Halibrand cast magnesium knock-off wheels, also the same as those used on the Cunninghams. These were shod with Firestone Super Sports racing tires, size 6.70-15 at the front, 7.60-15 at the rear. These tires put a foot-

Top photos: *Hand-building the SS under Zora Duntov's watchful supervision.* **Above left:** *The fiberglass Mule at speed on GM test track.* **Above left and below:** *Duntov in SS with wild bubble top attached, at Sebring in 1957, and reunited with his creation at Laguna Seca in 1987.*

specifications

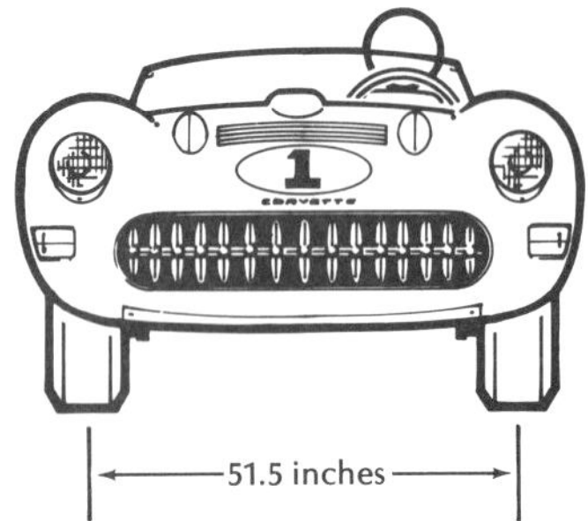
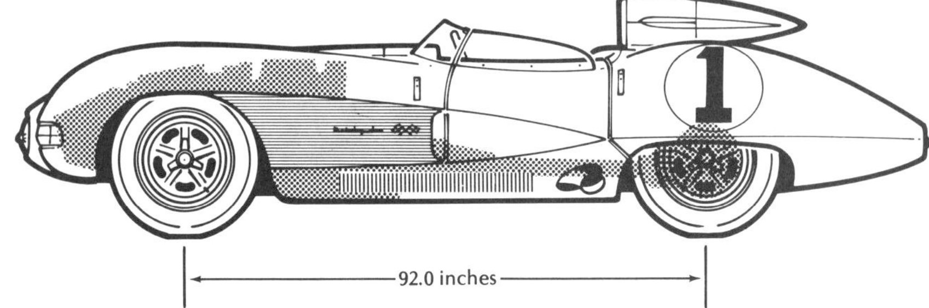

1957 Chevrolet Corvette Super Sports

Price	$100,000 plus to build; never offered for sale
Options	None

ENGINE

Type	90-degree V-8
Bore and stroke	3.875 inches x 3.00 inches
Displacement	283 cubic inches, 4,640 cc
Compression ratio	9.0:1 (11.0:1 optional)
HP @ rpm	310 @ 6,000
Torque @ rpm	295 @ 4,400
Valves	OHV
Valve lifters	Mechanical
Main bearings	5
Induction system	Rochester constant-flow mechanical fuel-injection
Lubrication system	Positive pressure
Exhaust system	Tuned-length, 40-inch individual headers merging to dual collectors, no mufflers
Electrical system	12 volt

CLUTCH

Type	Single dry plate
Diameter	10.5 inches
Actuation	Mechanical, foot pedal

TRANSMISSION

Type	4-speed selective, tunnel mounted selector
Ratios: 1st	1.87:1
2nd	1.54:1
3rd	1.22:1
4th	1.00:1
Reverse	1.87:1

DIFFERENTIAL

Type	Halibrand quick-change
Ratio	2.63 to 4.80, 3.87:1 at Sebring
Drive axles	Semi-floating
Torque medium	Four trailing arms

STEERING

Type	Saginaw recirculating ball
Ratio, overall	12:1
Turns lock to lock	2.5
Power-assisted	No

BRAKES

Type	4-wheel hydraulic Chrysler Center-Plane 2LS Al-Fin drum, inboard at rear
Drum diameter	12 inches
Effective area	376.9 square inches
Power assist	No

CONSTRUCTION

Frame	Multi-tubular steel space frame
Body construction	All magnesium
Body type	Two-door, two-passenger roadster, removable plexiglass hardtop

SUSPENSION

Front	Independent, long and short control arms, coilover spring/shock absorber units, anti-roll bar
Rear	DeDion, four trailing arms, coilover spring/shock absorber units
Tires	Firestone Super Sports, 6.50-15 front, 7.60-15 rear
Wheels	Halibrand cast magnesium, 5.00-15, knock-off hubs
Shock absorbers	Delco direct-acting tubular, in unit with coil springs

WEIGHTS AND MEASURES

Wheelbase	92 inches
Overall length	168 inches
Front track	51.5 inches
Rear track	51.5 inches
Dry weight	1,850 pounds

CAPACITIES

Crankcase	8 quarts
Cooling system	18 quarts
Fuel tank	43 gallons

CALCULATED DATA

HP/c.i.d.	1.096
Pounds/HP	6.6
Pounds/c.i.d.	6.53
PSI, brakes	4.9
Production, this series/body style	1

This page: SS rear styling is extremely clean and unfussy. *Facing page, top:* Fuel-injected 310-hp V-8 sits well back in chassis for excellent balance. *Below:* Rear view mirror is mounted in pod for better aerodynamics.

CORVETTE SS

print about 4.5 inches wide on the ground...narrower than a Honda Civic tire, today. Imagine going 150 mph with just a few square inches of indifferent rubber to connect you to the track!

The rear brakes were placed inboard, flanking the differential, and looking almost exactly like the similarly finned inboard drums of the Mercedes 300SL. Air ducting from the front and rear grilles was routed to cool the brakes, which used special Cera-metallic linings and an unusual vacuum-servo brake booster with mercury-switch proportioning valve that was supposed to prevent rear-wheel lock up.

The prototype shop fabricated a 43-gallon fuel tank from fiberglass, fantastically shaped to fit around the rear frame tubes and fitted with twin electric fuel pumps. To protect the magnesium body from stone damage, they had to build inner fender liners, front and rear. Overall weight came out to a claimed 1,850 pounds dry, which was just about the same as the new Ferrari Testa Rossa, but a couple of hundred pounds lighter than either the Devin SS or Reventlow Scarab, both similar size sports/racers with the same Corvette V-8 and running gear as the SS.

By Christmas 1956, it was obvious that the SS would just barely be finished in time for Sebring in March. Despite strict orders not to, Duntov started work on a second chassis that could be used for pre-race testing. Ultimately, his engineering group constructed five frames, only two of which were turned into running automobiles.

The first chassis was completed and given to the Styling group to be turned into the actual finished race car. The second chassis was built using identical components, but in an extremely rough-hewn form. A hurried fiberglass body had been laid-up to use for wind tunnel testing, and as Duntov says, "We put the body built for the aerodynamic tests on the spare chassis we had constructed on the side." Originally, the fiberglass car was fitted with a stock carbureted 283 V-8, and used for testing suspension components at the test track contained within the GM Tech Center.

When John Fitch had been on the Mercedes team, they had always had such a test car, which they referred to as "Das Mule." Fitch christened Duntov's test car the Mule, and the name stuck. As Fitch said at the time, "The car is a combination of the ugly duckling and the poor little rich girl who has never been to finishing school, but she *flies!*"

As it turned out, Duntov — who had been a top rank racing driver before

joining Chevrolet — covered some 2,000 high-speed miles in the Mule, both at the GM track and at Sebring. As faults were found, they would be corrected on the Mule, then the real SS would be modified to match. This testing went on right up until the day before the race at Sebring...when it became painfully obvious that the SS would be lucky to make the start at all.

By then, Duntov had whipped the Mule into a pretty decent racing car. With all its cobbled-up bits and pieces, cast-iron cylinder heads and fiberglass body, the Mule weighed about 150 pounds more than the mostly alloy SS...but it was surprisingly competitive once practice started at Sebring.

Fitch and Duntov were rivals of a sort ...both experienced racer/inventor/engineers angling for control of Corvette racing. Fitch had angered Duntov by taking the production Corvettes to Sebring in 1956 despite Duntov's objections, so when it came time to hire drivers for the SS, Duntov deliberately overlooked Fitch. Fitch was already involved with the three-car Corvette team for Sebring — the SR-2, plus two production coupes — to be driven by the most famous Corvette racers in the country. Pete Lovely and Paul O'Shea had the SR-2, with Dr. Dick Thompson and Gaston Andrey in one coupe and Dale Duncan, "Honest John" Kilborn and Jim Jeffords in the other.

Instead of John Fitch, Duntov actually put together a deal with the greatest racing driver of his time, the greatest of all time, Juan Manuel Fangio. He then tried to sign up Stirling Moss, Fangio's chief rival, but Moss declined in favor of Maserati. Instead, Chevrolet made a contract with Carroll Shelby, who at least had the advantage of being American, even if he was trying to build a road-racing career in Europe.

As race day came closer and there was still no sign of a car to drive, first Fangio and then Shelby asked to be released from their contracts. Both signed on with Maserati. This happened on Mon-

CORVETTE SS

day, March 18, with the race scheduled to start just five days later. At the time, few people in or outside General Motors expected that the SS would even appear at Sebring.

John Fitch claims he had stayed away from the SS project, because he could see it was going to have problems from the very beginning. "Ed Cole was telling me about this car in the fall of 1956. He asked me to drive it at Sebring, and he said it was all ready to go. This was a pleasant surprise, I thought, all ready in plenty of time.

"Later, I found out that when Cole said 'ready,' he meant 'styled.' Bill Mitchell had drawn the body exterior... that's all that had been done. I went to the Tech Center to see the car, and Zora was just starting to build the space frame. It was a terrible disappointment, and I determined to concentrate on the production Corvette GT coupes instead."

With only a few days to go, Ed Cole persuaded Fitch to drive the SS, when and if it arrived. Fitch suggested the Italian veteran, Piero Taruffi, as his co-driver. In his autobiography, *Works Racer*, Taruffi explained, "At two o'clock in the morning on March 19, 1957, I was awakened by a telephone call from the United States. Still half asleep, I managed to gather that they wished me to drive a Chevrolet Corvette in the Sebring Twelve Hours. I replied that if I found two return tickets to Miami waiting for me at the Rome office of Pan-American Airlines next morning, I should be happy to go. And that is how my wife and I went to Miami and from there to Sebring."

John Fitch practiced with the Mule at

the end of the week, while Taruffi was flying from Italy and the SS was riding in a truck from Detroit. According to Zora Duntov, "The SS arrived just a day before the race. Stylists were still working on it in the transport van on the way to Florida. They told me, 'It must meet General Motors' standards as to appearance.' "

John Fitch managed to get the Mule down to a lap of three minutes, 32 seconds for the 5.2-mile Sebring track. Piero Taruffi, still groggy from his marathon flight from Rome and unfamiliar with the Sebring course, lapped at 3:35. The Chevrolet people were relatively pleased, because Mike Hawthorne's official lap record, set with a Jaguar D-type in 1956, was 3:29.6

In practice, however, Fangio lowered

the record to 3:25.8 with the 4.5-liter Maserati, followed by Musso's Ferrari Testa Rossa at 3:26.0, Moss's 3.0-liter Maserati at 3:26.8, dePortago's Ferrari at 3:27.3 and Peter Collins's at 3:27.5. Fangio's teammate Jean Behra clocked 3:27.8, just two seconds slower than Il Maestro, in the same car. Dozens of other cars lapped faster than Fitch in the Mule, including a 2.5-liter Maserati with half the displacement and only 220 horsepower.

Disappointed, on Friday afternoon Zora Duntov asked both Fangio and Moss to try the Mule for a few laps. Moss turned a 3.28:2, and in the manner of all racers said, "I can cut two or three seconds off that if I need to." Fangio turned 3:27.2, a full five seconds quicker than John Fitch in the same car. And as any racer will tell you, five seconds a lap is a lifetime in a sport where success is measured in hundredths.

Writing in the August 1957 issue of *Sports Cars Illustrated*, Karl Ludvigsen pointed out, "The moral of this is that (A) the SS Corvette is potentially one of the fastest sports cars in the world and (B) it won't do a bit of good unless they can sign up some Class A drivers."

Most of the Chevrolet team's time at Sebring was spent posing for publicity photos with the still-untried SS. John Fitch with Ed Cole. Zora Duntov with Ed Cole. John Fitch and Zora Duntov with Ed Cole. John Fitch with Zora Duntov. John Fitch with the SS. Ed Cole with the SS. Zora Duntov with the SS. Finally, in the last practice session on the Friday afternoon before the race, Fitch was able to take a few easy laps in the actual SS.

The verdict? "Intolerable." The fiberglass bodywork on the Mule was an insulator. The magnesium bodywork on

courtesy GM Photographic

*Top: John Fitch, 1957 Corvette team driver with the SS at Laguna Seca in 1987. **Facing page:** Fitch in the SS 30 years before. **Above:** Chasing but not catching competitors at Sebring in 1957. **Facing page:** Giving the old warrior some exercise under Fitch's guidance at Laguna last year.*

34

the SS was a conductor. The great curving headers literally wrapped around the driver's feet, the exhaust went right under his leg. In the steamy atmosphere of central Florida, under a broiling sun, the SS cockpit was like a sauna. Duntov had the cove panels removed and fiberglass insulation packed inside the cockpit.

Even worse, while the brakes on the Mule were perfect, the front brakes of the SS operated erratically...making the car a dangerous handful to drive. The crew worked overnight transferring parts from the Mule to the SS, and John Fitch took it out early Saturday morning to try. He ran it up and down the airport runways adjacent to the course, jamming the brakes on to try and get them to pull evenly. In the process, he locked the brakes and flat-spotted the front tires, but with only 15 minutes before the start, there was no time to change them.

In those far-off days, there was no qualifying in endurance races. Grid positions — and car numbers — were assigned by engine displacement, with modified cars gridded ahead of production cars of the same engine size. Thus the SS was Number 1, and started from the pole. The SR-2 was 2, the production Corvette coupes 3 and 4, followed by the field, many of which were actually faster cars.

The start was what was called a "LeMans Start," in which the drivers lined up behind a line 50 yards from their cars, which were diagonally parked side-by-side. When the American flag was dipped to start the race, they sprinted across the track, leaped into the cars and accelerated off. Exciting LeMans starts finally became passe when it took two helpers and five min-

utes to buckle the driver into his six-point seat belts, hook up his communications and cool-suit lines, arm restraints, helmet-restraint and Gatorade sipping hose. The last LeMans start at LeMans was in 1969.

By comparison, when John Fitch pattered across the cracked Sebring concrete at 10:11 AM, March 23, 1957, he stepped over the bottom-hinged SS door without opening it, fastened his lap belt as he ground the starter and accelerated away, the car already parked in gear. The two production Corvette coupes were the first away, side-by-side, but they were passed by Peter Collins's Ferrari before the first corner. Collins led the first lap, followed by Moss's Maserati, Phil Hill and Masten Gregory in their Ferraris, Jean Behra's Maserati

and then John Fitch, a splendid sixth in the SS.

After the third lap, Fitch pulled into the pits, to have the two flat-spotted front tires replaced. He then went out and turned a 3:29.8, the fastest lap the real SS would hit at Sebring. By comparison, Jean Behra set a new lap record of 3:24 with the 400-horsepower Maserati 450S, before turning it over to Fangio after three hours, with an incredible two-lap lead on the second-place car.

By then, the SS was laps behind. Mechanics in the pit had replaced a coil wire, and then Fitch had replaced the coil itself out on the course. Then the engine started overheating. Finally, the rubber bushings connecting the rear axle lower trailing arms to the frame split from being overtightened when the chassis was assembled. The tires started to hit the fenders on corners, and what with erratic brakes and uncontrollable handling, Fitch made an executive decision to retire the SS after 22 laps.

As Fitch tells it, "The race was a disaster. The SS had problems, insurmountable problems. I had driven the car only 22 laps within three or four hours, because we spent most of the time in the pits working on the car. Finally, I came into the pits and said, 'The car is unmanageable. It is dangerous to everyone. It dodges around unpredictably, and all I can do is aim it and hope it will go where I want it. I don't even want Taruffi to get into it, because he has no experience with the car in this condition.'

"Ed Cole was furious with me. He was busy having his picture taken with the SS while the car was in the pits. He said, 'We must go ahead and finish the race, with or without you.'

CORVETTE SS

"Against my wishes, my friend Piero Taruffi — who was a wonderful engineer and excellent driver — was sent out into race traffic. He made one slow lap in the SS. Then he rolled into the pits and removed his helmet. Zora and Ed Cole rushed to the side of the car. 'Withdraw the car,' he said."

After 12 hours, Behra/Fangio in their 4.5-liter Maserati were still two laps ahead of teammates Stirling Moss and Harry Schell with a 3.0-liter Maserati. Behra/Fangio led every lap, broke the lap record and won at a record-breaking speed. Mike Hawthorne and Ivor Bueb were five laps behind in third, driving a Jaguar D-type owned by Briggs Cunningham, the American East Coast Jaguar distributor. Americans Gregory and Brero were fourth with a Ferrari, Hansgen and Woods fifth with another Cunningham Jaguar.

The production Corvette team, with John Fitch back as manager after the SS broke, went on to a great success. Dr. Dick Thompson and Gaston Andrey were twelfth overall, but first in their GT class. The matching coupe, driven by Duncan/Kilborn/Jeffords, was second in GT, fifteenth overall, followed by the SR-2 in sixteenth, third in GT, driven by Lovely/O'Shea.

Prepared well ahead of time by Red Byron and Fitch, drawing on their experience from the year before, the GT cars had been practicing at Sebring weeks ahead of time; there had been two spare practice cars and the drivers had been molded into a congenial team. The contrast with the chaotic SS program couldn't have been more dramatic.

Surprisingly, Ed Cole was not discouraged. John Fitch wrote him a letter after Sebring, in which he suggested some improvements for the SS before LeMans, including a moveable decklid "air brake" like the Mercedes 300SLR had pioneered at LeMans in 1955. Fitch suggested this be coupled with moveable flaps that would open from the body sides to channel air to the brakes during braking, then retract under acceleration.

Cole himself ordered Harry Barr and Duntov to start work on desmodromic valves for the Chevrolet V-8, also similar to those used on the Mercedes 300SLR. This would allow them to use 9,000 rpm as a redline, at which point the 283 V-8 would produce 400 horsepower, enough to be competitive with the 400-horsepower Maserati which had won at Sebring. In the meantime, Duntov was to complete the three remaining frames. The intention was to show up at LeMans with a four-car SS team, plus the faithful Mule.

It was not to be. At the February meeting of the Automobile Manufacturers Association, Red Curtice, the president of General Motors, proposed a resolution that the AMA "recommends to member companies that they take no part in automobile racing or other competitive events involving tests of speed, and that they refrain from suggesting speed in passenger car advertising or publicity." The resolution was passed unanimously at the April meeting, and went into effect on June 1, 1957. *Les Vingt-quatres heures du Mans* started on June 10.

Ironically enough, the Scots Ecurie Ecosse team brought five 3.8-liter D-type Jaguars to LeMans, and finished 1-2-3-4-6, in perhaps their finest hour. As a direct result, the French-dominated Commission Sportive International voted in August to restrict entrants in international endurance races to less than 3.0 liters. This eliminated not only the Jaguars, but also the big Maseratis and Ferraris...and Corvettes. This is why the classic sports/racers of the late fifties — Ferrari Testa Rossa, Aston Martin DBR/1, Maserati Tipo 61 — are all 3.0 liters or less.

The combination of the AMA ban on racing and the CSI ban on over 3.0-liter cars effectively put Chevrolet out of the racing business. In May, the three unbuilt SS frames were scrapped. The Mule was stuck in the GM Styling warehouse on Twelve Mile Road in Warren, across from the Tech Center, along with a bunch of old styling studies and Motorama showcars.

The Mule remained there in exile for two years, until Bill Mitchell rescued it and rebodied it into the original Sting Ray racer, with which Dick Thompson won an SCCA National Championship. Today, the Mule/Sting Ray is still owned by GM Styling, and still resides in a warehouse on Twelve Mile Road, except for rare moments, such as last August's Monterey Historic, when it was reunited with Dick Thompson for the first time in nearly 30 years. GM Styling's Kenny Eschebach, who has cared for the Sting Ray its whole life, says he spent two months prepping it for Monterey.

Zora Duntov had the SS rebuilt after Sebring, and installed the 2.80:1 differential it would have carried at LeMans. Bill Mitchell fitted it with body-color covers for the headlamps and driving lights. He also gave it the *monoposto* windscreen with which it was originally designed. In this form, Duntov took it to General Motors Phoenix proving grounds in December of 1958, where it lapped the five-mile test track at an average speed of 183 mph...exactly the top speed which would have been needed on the Mulsanne Straight at LeMans.

Two months later, Zora and the SS were invited by Bill France to christen the newly built 2.5-mile Daytona International Speedway. Duntov lapped the tri-oval at 155 mph, just about the same speed the NASCAR drivers reached in the following week's 1959 Daytona 500, won by Lee Petty's Oldsmobile at an average speed of 135 mph...including pit stops and caution flags.

The SS was then stuck away in the Styling warehouse for years, until it was finally converted back to two-seater configuration, cleaned up and presented to the Indianapolis Speedway Museum.

The view that Chevrolet hoped other race cars would have of the SS. In actual competition it proved nearly unmanageable at speed.

SS is very easy to drive, but in inexperienced hands it can turn around and bite without warning.

Ironically, it was then stored in the basement at Indy, for lack of space. When Chevrolet decided to bring it to Laguna Seca for the Monterey Historic, they had to first borrow it back from Indy, promising not to drive it!

Driving Impressions

After years of sitting in Indianapolis, the SS was in sorry shape. Retired GM engineer Lou Cutitta, who helped build the SS 30 years ago, reportedly spent six months and $50,000 to restore the SS to running condition before Monterey. Even then, it was barely driveable. Cutitta had to fiddle with the fuel injection before I could get it started and drive it across the paddock before the weekend started, and as John Fitch put it the next day, "The SS needs a lot of help. A lot of things still aren't right. You drive it like a basket of eggs."

At Monterey Historic, Chevy PR guy Jim Hall took the SS for an unauthorized lap around Laguna Seca, and managed to spin in the hairpin. After that, John Fitch was the only driver allowed behind the wheel, giving rides to Zora Duntov, Chevy general manager Bob Burger and other luminaries. At least, he was the only one to drive it until the end of the weekend when I idled it a mile or so back across the infield, where it was loaded back on the truck for its trip

home to Indianapolis...where no doubt, it will be allowed to deteriorate once again.

What's the SS like to drive? As you'd expect, very much like any other Chevy-powered sports/racer from the fifties. These cars have so much horsepower and torque for their light weight, you can just idle off from rest at 1,000 rpm, with none of the clutch-slipping finesse needed to launch many high-strung race cars. Once you're moving, the steering is very light, the ride surprisingly good, and at least at low speeds, the brakes are fine. And of course, the Borg-Warner four-speed is probably the easiest-shifting gearbox ever bolted behind a V-8.

Unlike most of these old V-8s, which are as tough as nails, the SS feels very delicate..."like a basket of eggs" describes it perfectly. You have to be careful opening and closing the doors, for fear of bending something, and it's a brave man indeed who would try to open the huge and wobbly hood unaided. Even in the paddock, I kept waiting for something to break...it feels like that kind of car.

Drive it through a crowd, and you can watch their heads swivel around as they hear you come up behind them, then the smiles break out on their faces. Nobody puts their hands over their ears

like they do when some of the smaller, more insistent racers go by, the ones whose exhaust will set the fillings in your teeth to vibrating.

When the SS goes by, you can see people happily bathing in that indescribable, low-pitched *whomp, whomp, whomp* of a Chevy V-8 with open pipes, solid lifters and a lot of valve overlap. What I remember most about the Corvette SS is the sound. The unforgettable sound. The sound of dreams...sadly, unfulfilled. □

Acknowledgements
Our thanks to Ralph Kramer, Nancy Libby and Jim Hall, Chevrolet Public Relations, Warren, Michigan; James Rooney, Chevrolet Public Relations, Floral Park, New York; Brian Wilson, GM Photographic, Warren, Michigan; Eric Dahlquist, The Vista Group, Van Nuys, California; Zora Arkus-Duntov and Lou Cutitta, Corvette Engineering (retired), Warren, Michigan; Bill Mitchell and Dick Henderson, GM Styling (retired), Warren, Michigan; Ken Eschebach and Dale Jacobson, GM Styling, Warren, Michigan; Steve Earle, Historic Motor Racing Association, Santa Barbara, California; Dr. Richard Thompson, Washington, DC; Stirling Moss, London, England. Our special thanks to John Fitch, Falls Village, Connecticut.

1957 FUEL INJECTION CORVETTE

283 cubes = 283 horsepower

   Originally published in Special Interest Autos #73, Jan.-Feb. 1983

by Dave Emanuel
photos by Roy Query

THIRTY YEARS have passed since Chevrolet Motor Division apprehensively introduced their first sports car. During the intervening years, economic, political and sociological turmoil has wrought immeasurable change upon the face of the nation, often obscuring the priorities that were paramount during previous decades.

So it is with the Corvette. In the beginning, it was little more than an experiment to determine whether a home-grown sports car could successfully compete with the European imports. In 1953, there was precious little indication that a long-term market existed for such a vehicle, but at least some of GM's executives had vision of sufficient acuity to read between the lines of market research reports. And over the years, their confidence in the Corvette project has been vindicated. The car is now a national institution.

Although it continues a tradition begun in 1953, recent incarnations are separated from their antecedents by a broad conceptual chasm; early Corvettes are sports cars, later models are grand touring machines. Given the current state-of-the-art, and immense popularity achieved by the Corvette, it is difficult to imagine that the marque once struggled for mere survival and almost died in infancy. Further, the significance of the engineering developments that set the Corvette on firm footing has been muddied by the waters of time.

During its embryonic years, America's only sports car suffered more than a few teething pains. Equipped with a six-cylinder engine and two-speed automatic transmission, and perched on a modified sedan chassis, the first models offered less than spine-tingling performance. And while the division's decision to cloak the car in a fiberglass, rather than steel body was laudable, quite some time was required to iron out production problems associated with the new material. Thus in attempting to lure sports car buyers with a product that lacked refinement, Chevrolet was knocking heads with relatively sophisticated European makes, specifically Jaguar, Austin-Healey and MG. The advantage enjoyed by these marques was further enhanced by a legacy of racing success, something the

Model year 1957 was when Chevrolet truly got the Corvette's act together. By combining the nicely restyled '56 body with the fire-breathing option of fuel injection they built a car which had begun in 1953 as a hesitant pussycat and transformed it to a snarling tiger.

Right: Many enthusiasts of the marque consider the '57 Corvette to be the most attractive car ever to wear that badge. Below: Taillamps are sunk in chromed nacelles; "bumpers" offered little protection from close encounters of the parking kind. Below right: Vette's dual exhausts exit through the bumpers. Bottom: Concave body side sweepspears began in 1956 and continued with some trim modifications through 1962.

1957 CORVETTE

Corvette was too new and anemic to achieve. This situation undoubtedly induced more than one buyer to opt for a British, rather than American two-seater.

On road courses, the 1953 and 1954 models were 98-pound weaklings, capable of little else besides having sand kicked in their faces. Muscles began to ripple during the following two years, but it wasn't until 1957 that the Corvette, now with broad shoulders and bulging biceps, began kicking its competition off the beach. Zora Arkus-Duntov, commonly known as the father of the Corvette, had begun working his engineering magic. And the United States had finally produced a world class sports car.

Among Corvette aficionados, 1957 stands as a high water mark and well it should; there can be little to dispute

that the quintessential Corvette was produced in that year. It was in 1957 that the original 265-cubic-inch V-8 was enlarged to 283 cubic inches, and fuel injection, a close ratio four-speed transmission, a special suspension and braking package and Positraction were all added to the option list. But of even greater significance, in its fuel injected form, the new 283 became the first American production engine to achieve a ratio of one horsepower per cubic inch of displacement. Chevrolet, seeking to capitalize on this fact, announced in its ads, "It is with considerable pride that Chevrolet invites you to examine an engineering advance of great significance, available on the 1957 Corvette. It is fuel injection, and in the Corvette V-8 it permits a level of efficiency hitherto unrealized in any American production car: *one horsepower for every cubic inch of displacement...283 hp!"*

Seeking to drive home the fact that the Corvette was indeed a thoroughbred sports car, the ad continued, "This is another major step in the creation of a proud new kind of car for America: a *genuine* sports car, as certified by its record in competition. But a *unique* sports car in its combination of moderate price, luxurious equipment and low cost maintenance with fiery performance, polo-pony responsiveness and granite stability on curves."

While the advertising copy smacks of hype, it was, in actuality, not far off the mark. The 283-hp fuel injected engine

did provide "fiery performance." In combination with a 4.11:1 rear axle and four-speed transmission, the powerplant propelled the car from zero to 60 mph in 5.7 seconds and from zero to 100 mph in 16.8 seconds. Standing start quarter mile figures were equally impressive as the car sprinted the distance in 14.3 seconds, reaching a speed of over 96 miles per hour. These performance figures were compiled by *Road & Track* magazine which went on to report, "An engine speed of 6500 is easily reached in fourth gear, equivalent to 132 mph with no allowance for tire expansion. With suitable gears the Corvette can approach 150 mph, as has been proven at Bonneville and at Daytona."

But in order to earn its bars within the sports car fraternity, the Corvette had to prove its mettle on the race track. Chevrolet was sensitive to this fact and

Top: The two magic words that mean one horsepower per cubic inch appear on the trunk lid. Above left: Gas filler is hidden away in front of left rear wheel well. Above center: High-styled wheel covers with "knock off" spinner added to Vette's sporty image. Above: Convertible top and optional hardtop were secured on the deck by chromed clamps. Left: Huge radio speaker outlet complements shape of speedo housing.

offered a $725 option tailored specifically for road racing. Known as Regular Production Option (RPO) 684, the package included higher rate front springs (340 as opposed to 300 pounds/inch), five-leaf rather than four-leaf rear springs, 13/16-inch-diameter front anti-roll bar, specially calibrated shock absorbers measuring 1⅜ inches rather than one inch in diameter, quicker steering (16.3:1 as opposed to the standard 21.0:1 ratio), Positraction rear axle, finned brake drums and ceramic/metallic brake linings. Wider wheels measuring 5.5 rather than 5.0 inches were available under RPO 276. By specifying the proper options, it was possible to order a car virtually race-ready, directly from the factory. (How times have changed.)

The race car image was further enhanced by the Corvette's record in competition—a first in GT class and a

specifications

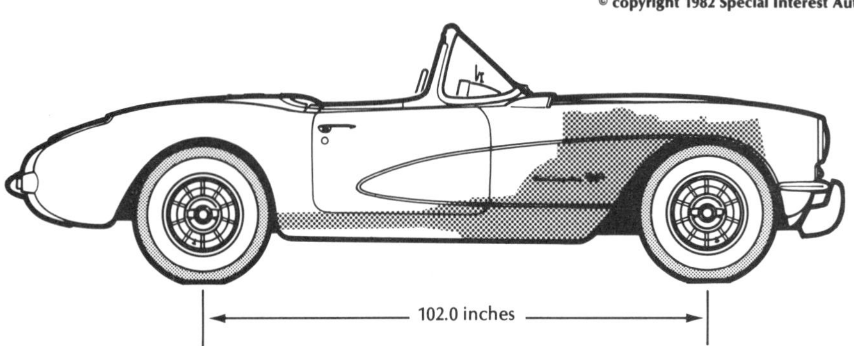

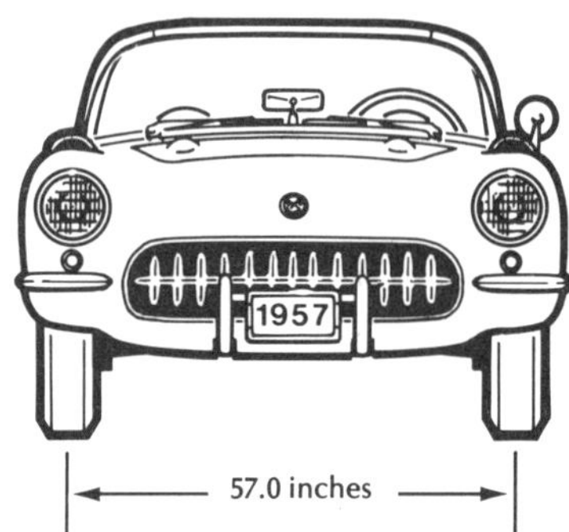

1957 Corvette

Base Price	$3909.52 f.o.b. St. Louis, MO
Optional equipment	Fuel injection, four-speed transmission, hardtop, "two-tone" paint, radio

ENGINE

Type	V-8 ohv
Bore & stroke	3.875 x 3.00
Displacement	283 cubic inches
Horsepower	283 @ 6200 rpm
Torque	290 @ 4400 rpm
Compression ratio	10.5:1
Induction system	Rochester Ramjet continuous flow fuel injection
Exhaust system	Dual, 2.0-inch o.d. exhaust pipes
Electrical system	12-volt battery/coil

TRANSMISSION

Type	4-speed manual
Ratios: 1st	2.20:1
2nd	1.66:1
3rd	1.31:1
4th	1:1

DIFFERENTIAL

Type	Hypoid semi-floating
Ratio	3.70:1 (3.55:1, 4.11:1 and 4.56:1 optional)

STEERING

Type	Semi-reversible, worm and ball bearing roller
Ratio	16.0:1 overall
Turns lock to lock	3.9
Turning circle	37 feet

BRAKES

Type	Hydraulic duo-servo cast iron drums 11 inches x 2.00 inches front, 11 inches x 1.75 inches rear
Total swept area	157 square inches (121 with H.D. brake option)
Lining material	Molded asbestos standard, sintered metal and ceramic optional heavy duty

CHASSIS & BODY

Construction	Welded box section frame with "X" crossmember
Body	Fiberglass 2-door roadster

SUSPENSION

Front	Independent SLA, coil springs, double-acting tubular shocks, anti-sway bar
Rear	Live axle with semi-elliptic leaf springs, double-acting tubular shocks, anti-sway bar with optional heavy duty option
Wheels	15-inch x 5-inch slotted steel disc
Tires	6.70 x 15-inch 4-ply rayon

WEIGHTS AND MEASURES

Wheelbase	102.0 inches
Overall length	168.0 inches
Overall height	51.9 inches
Overall width	70.5 inches
Front tread	57.0 inches
Rear tread	59.0 inches
Curb weight	2849 pounds

PERFORMANCE

Maximum speed	132
Acceleration 0-50	4.7 seconds
0-60	5.7 seconds
Standing start ¼ mile	14.3 seconds and 96 mph
Fuel economy	11-16 mpg

1957 CORVETTE

twelfth and fifteenth overall at the 1957 edition of the 12 Hours of Sebring. A Corvette also won the season-opening sports car race at New Smyrna Beach, Florida, defeating a Jaguar XK-140, a Thunderbird and a Mercedes-Benz 300SL in the process. Other victories included a 1-2-3-4 finish in the stock production category at Nassau Speed Weeks, the SCCA B Production class championship, and at Daytona Beach, the car dominated the C Production class placing first, second and third in both standing start acceleration and flying mile competition. A winning speed of 131.941 was posted in the latter category.

By mid-year the 1957 Corvette, especially the fuel injected version, was well on its way to becoming a classic.

Obviously, 283 horsepower @ 6200 rpm was not every buyer's idea of nirvana and for the more effete driver, Chevrolet offered several alternatives. The base engine, which was fitted with a mild hydraulic cam, Carter WCFB four-barrel and 9.5:1 compression ratio, bore a rating of 220 hp @ 4800 rpm; with optional dual WCFB carburetors, the horsepower rating rose to 245 @ 5000 rpm. Just as all the lower horsepower engines shared the same hydraulic cam, the top options were fitted with the identical "competition" mechanical lifter grind. When combined with dual Carter WCFBs, the "Duntov" cam was responsible for 270 hp @ 6000 rpm; with fuel injection, the rating jumped to 283 hp @ 6200 rpm.

All engines were available with either three or four-speed manual transmissions or two-speed Powerglide automatic. Both of the manual gearboxes were of the close ratio variety with gear sets of 2.21:1, 1.32:1 and 1:1 and 2.20:1, 1.66:1, 1.31:1 and 1:1 respectively for the three and four-speed models. A tubular driveshaft connected the transmission to the rear axle where ratios ranged from 3.55:1 to 4.56:1 with either conventional or Positraction differential carrier.

In all, six exterior colors were offered —Onyx Black, Venetian Red, Polo White, Arctic Blue, Cascade Green and Aztec Copper. An optional paint treatment consisted of either Shoreline Beige or Silver Metallic, rather than the body color, being applied to the scallop which extended along the doors and front fenders. Interior colors were listed as Shoreline Beige or Venetian Red.

With exceptional performance, handling capability and visual appeal, the 1957 Corvette has fulfilled the prophecy of its builder: "It is our intention to

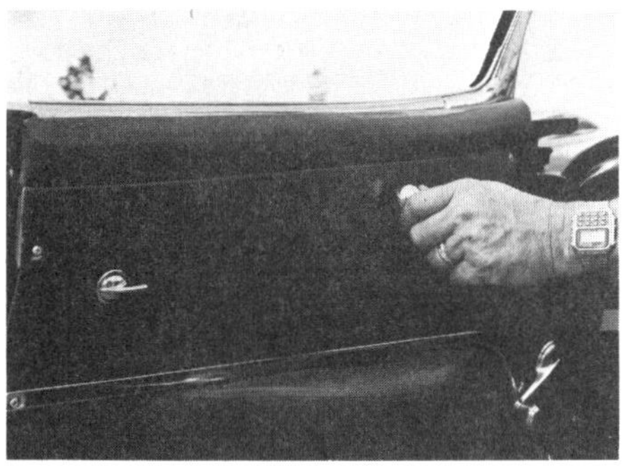
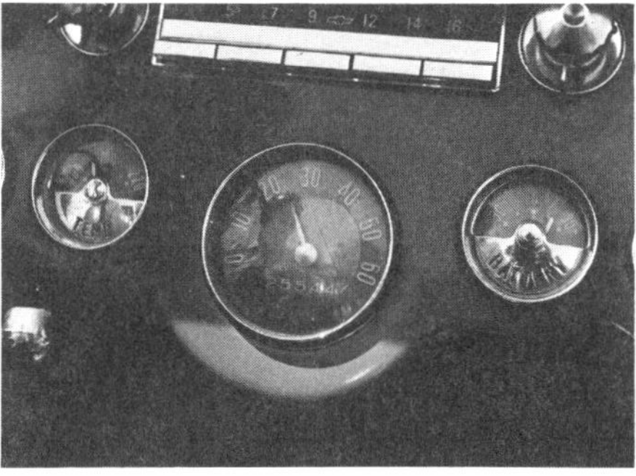
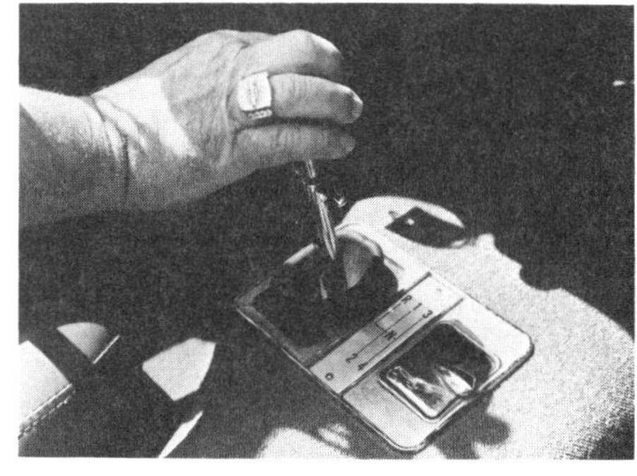

Left: Good looks aside, the true allure of the '57 fuelie is in the driving. Breathtaking performance all the way through the power band awaits the command of your right foot. Below left: Doors open with convenient push-pull knob. Below center: Tachometer occupies exact center of dash; not the most convenient spot for a quick reading of the revs. Below: With all the power on tap a four-speed box seems almost unnecessary, but it was in keeping with the desire to make the Corvette a thoroughbred sports car. Bottom:The durable 283 V-8 could be ordered with a relatively tame 220 hp all the way up to the unprecedented one horsepower per cubic inch version.

make of the Corvette a classic car, one of those rare and happy milestones in the history of automotive design." Chevrolet had indeed created a classic—distinctive of line, limited in number and revered by serious collectors and casual enthusiasts alike. It's a sad fact that a mere 6339 samples of the 1957 edition were produced (only 240 with fuel injection), and of these, many have long since departed for the great wrecking yard in the sky. But somewhere, tucked away in a barn, a star is waiting to be discovered.

Driving Impressions

Whenever conversation turns to fuel-injected Corvettes, my memory flips back to an evening in 1963 when a 1957 "fuelie" went head-to-head with a high-powered motorcycle. The image of the bike has long since faded from my cerebral cavity; I can't even remember what make it was, although I'd bet it was a Harley. But I remember the black and silver 'Vette as if I had seen it just yesterday. With the paint shimmering beneath the street lights, the Corvette rolled out of its parking space and moved alongside the bike. Waiting to enter the road, its fuel injection unit emitted that unmistakable whistle while the mechanical lifters clattered like so many cymbals in a symphony of machination. It is the sight and sound of the car more than the race itself that remains so strongly implanted in my

memory—it had a certain, unforgettable charisma, somewhat akin to that of a mythical princess. And it beckoned as coyly, staying close enough to touch, but always just out of reach for all but a fortunate few. This is perhaps the reason that fuel injected Corvettes in general and 1957 models in particular have achieved such great popularity.

As I climbed behind the wheel of the driveReport car, the memories of that night 20 years ago came flooding back. All the right sounds and sights were present; the only things lacking were the motorcycle and some of the hair that used to call the top of my head home.

But if the 'Vette was impressive in 1963, it must have been awesome the year it was built. Letting my mind wander, I could envision what it must have been like when a proud owner had just taken delivery of a brand new 1957 fuel injected, four-speed Corvette. At the time it had to be the fastest production car on the road, and I'm sure it was displayed all over town with the pride and enthusiasm usually demonstrated only by a new mother showing off her progeny. The mind games were fun, but when I began to seriously evaluate the car in practical terms, I noticed that the princess had more than a few warts.

Carburetion versus Injection

A few years ago, before the Corvette restoration movement shifted into high gear, Rochester fuel injection units were readily available for $75-$150. Generally, all other things being equal, the older the model the lower the price. This state of affairs was brought about by a lack of understanding on the part of Corvette owners. As soon as an injection unit became the least bit troublesome, it would be replaced with a carburetor and intake manifold. The fuel injection equipment would subsequently be sold for whatever it would bring. Today, those same units bring from $1500 to $2000.

An alternative to fuel injection, available from 1956 through 1961, was twin four-barrel carburetors. Equipped with the same mechanical lifter cam as the injected engine, the dual four-barrel arrangement was rated at 270-horsepower. Some people have disputed that rating stating that Chevrolet, seeking to spotlight fuel injection, was overly conservative when applying horsepower figures to the carbureted engine.

While it may not have all the charisma of fuel injection, a dual four-barrel induction system has a magical ring all its own. Since the carburetors were relatively trouble-free, many original 270-horsepower Corvettes have survived intact. One example is the 1957 model owned by John Brock of Houston, Texas. An active member of a local Corvette club, Brock raced his concours-winning '57 in autocross competition until quite recently. "It was a real kick," says Brock. "All I had to do was change wheels and tires and go. I think that part of the fun of owning an older car is driving it—not just letting it sit around like a hangar queen. I did fairly well with the '57, but it began to pick up a few too many rock chips, so I don't race it anymore. But I still enjoy driving it."

1957 CORVETTE

While it is now quite in vogue to excoriate the caliber of newer automobiles vis-a-vis their ancestors, there is much to be said for later model Corvettes. Certainly with air conditioning, AM-FM/stereo tape and a plethora of power accessories, they lack the simplicity of the older models. They also lack the throttle response and raw feel of horsepower that is characteristic of a Chevy small block fitted with a mechanical lifter camshaft. But the newer Corvettes are generally much more enjoyable to drive. They offer more room in the cockpit, demonstrably superior handling and ride comfort and significantly better braking capability.

Much of the 1957 models' handling potential is compromised by original equipment type bias ply tires. The car does go around corners well, albeit with more lean than should be present in a sports car, but a set of high performance radial tires, although viewed as anathema by purists, would make a world of difference.

Then again, one doesn't usually expect a 26-year-old car to live up to current state-of-the-art standards. The fact that the '57 Corvette comes so close as to invite comparison is testimony to the high caliber of its design. But the true essence of the car is not in its undercarriage but its under-hood equipage. With the exhaust pipes reverberating to the engine's 750 rpm staccato idle, the whistle of air flowing through the fuel injection and the rat-a-tat of pushrods rapping against rocker arms, anyone who appreciates the beauty of a highly tuned powerplant is immediately enraptured. And as you spend more time behind the wheel, the captivation grows greater, prompting

Upper right: There's plenty of leg room inside, and the "waffle" pattern semi-bucket seats are much plusher than the Corvette's European counterparts. *Right:* Push-button on metal band between seats allows access to top storage area. *Below:* Vette has one of the most symmetrical dashboards ever designed.

Left: All graceful, sweeping curves in the rear, it looks like it's going 100 even when standing still. *Below left:* Grille design on '57s was carried over from original '53 Corvette styling. *Below:* Fuel injection identification plates are also carried in sweep spears. *Center left:* Airscoops in front fenders are non-functional; they're perhaps the only piece of styling gimmickry in an otherwise sensationally sleek design. *Below center:* Installing or removing optional factory hardtop is a two-person operation. *Bottom:* Rear appearance is "just right"; smooth, sensual and purposeful.

you to forget the world of emissions controls and emasculating government regulations.

Pulling away easily from a dead stop, the engine's responsiveness and eagerness to accelerate leaves no doubt that the true performance potential has been barely tapped. Moving the shift lever through the gears as you accelerate, the feeling of power diminishes only slightly thanks to the closeness of gear ratios. Once in fourth gear, 60 miles per hour is quickly reached, even though you've conservatively applied your right foot to the accelerator pedal. With a more vigorous driving style, 0-60 mph times fall in the low six second range and after 17 seconds of full throttle driving, the speedometer is swinging past the 100 mile per hour mark. The engine, transmission and rear axle seem to enjoy a symbiotic relationship, all working in harmony to yield a result that's greater than the sum of the parts.

Although a removable hardtop was optionally available, it borders on sacrilege to drive an early model Corvette in anything other than open roadster form—to do otherwise is analagous to dressing Bo Derek in baggy overalls. Driving with the top down may leave you wind blown and feeling a bit gritty, but that's all part of what driving a classic Corvette is all about—it's a matter of essentials, a man and his machine. Once the bond is made, nothing else seems to matter. □

Acknowledgements and Bibliography

The Best of Corvette News, *edited by Karl Ludvigsen;* Corvette America's Star-Spangled Sports Car *by Karl Ludvigsen;* Road & Track, *various issues;* Corvettes Technically Speaking, *by Michael G. Harrison. Special thanks to Bob McDorman, Bob McDorman Chevrolet, Canal Winchester, Ohio; John Brock, Brock's Collision Repair, Houston, Texas; and Bob Fitch, Houston, Texas.*

1962 CORVETTE

LAST OF THE CLASSIC CORVETTES, FIRST OF THE 327s

by John G. Tennyson
photos by the author

S INCE the early days of motoring, Americans have been intrigued with sports cars and their racing heritage. The early American runabouts and sport roadsters — such as Mercer and Stutz — are a recognized part of our automotive history. But by the twenties and thirties, most sporty cars of American vintage, though fast, were too large to be considered true sports cars in the same sense as their European contemporaries.

Not until postwar years, with MG and Jaguar leading the way, was American interest in the classic two-seater sports car rekindled on an even larger scale, and Corvette, in the fifties, then proceeded to capitalize on their popularity by making the sports car an American institution as well.

Perhaps more than any other postwar make, Corvette has influenced the later development of other more youthful and sporty American cars, such as the "pony" and "muscle" cars of the sixties, while remaining the most revered of them all.

But the first Corvettes were not always so popular. Revolutionary as a production car with fiberglass construction when first introduced in 1953, the Corvette was still found too

Originally published in Special Interest Autos #116, Mar.-Apr. 1990

Driving Impressions

Our driveReport Corvette is the top carbureted model produced in 1962, the 340-horsepower version with the four-speed tranny, heavy duty suspension and brakes, and a Positraction 4.11:1 rear end. The car has most of the convenience options of the catalog that year, except electric windows and power soft top.

On the road the car is, in a word, fast! We did not put this original example through the kind of tests such cars were subjected to by car magazines when new, but driving around the hills near Portland, Oregon, we obtained a pretty good sampling of this car's road manners in most situations.

The car is almost too fast from a standing start in ordinary traffic; other cars just cannot get out of the way. The Corvette eats up the hills, even in fourth gear. The 4.11:1 rear end allows use of fourth gear as low as 35 mph without lugging, providing both good low- and high-end performance. Of course, we won't talk about gas mileage; that was not a consideration in 1962.

The four-speed shifter is fully synchronized and easy to operate without excessive throw.

Good brakes are a necessity on a car with this kind of muscle, and the optional heavy-duty drum brakes, with power assist not yet available, bring this 3,000-pound beast to a straight and sure stop. No wonder seat belts were standard!

The ride is very firm, and the cornering fairly flat. The Corvette steers pretty much on target, though with some understeer. The steering wheel is large and nearly perpendicular to the floor — but still provides good leverage in fast maneuvers. On bumpy back roads, the heavy-duty suspension produces a fairly rough ride for those used to softer sprung cars, though driver control is still excellent.

Gauges are all very legible from the driver's seat, and most controls are within easy reach. The passenger grab bar and large door armrests are a very nice touch. The white-knobbed inside door handles, however, a carryover from earlier models, seem somewhat out of place on this kind of car.

The soft top is easily raised or lowered by one person. But the 55-pound detachable hardtop is another story. It takes two to lift into place or remove, though it is not so heavy as awkward. The top does provide a tight factory fit when bolted into place and looks like a genuine hardtop.

Rear bumpers — even though fastened to the frame and aesthetically pleasing — seem fragile and useless in the event of even a small bump. Front bumpers look only slightly more substantial. The trunk has surprising room for a sports car. Despite lack of depth, the trunk is wide and flat, with a spare tire which fits in a well under the floor mat and inside taillamp protectors, a new feature for '62. This was the last Corvette with a conventional trunk lid.

All in all, the '62 Corvette is impressive, even in light of more modern sports cars. Its fit and finish are superb, its styling "classic," and most of all its power is exhilarating.

The driveReport Corvette was originally purchased in May 1962 in Denver, Colorado, and has seen five owners. The second owner sold the car to a Dodge City, Kansas, man in 1977 with only 45,000 miles on the clock. The '62 again traded hands in '79, but the airline pilot who owned the car for the next ten years put on only 2,000 miles, mostly in moving to California. The car now has some 49,000.

For the current owner, John Milliken, Jr., of Lake Oswego, Oregon, purchase of the Corvette in early 1989 was the final achievement of a lifelong dream, a dream held since college days when he envied those "older" guys who could afford the '62 when new. Since that time, John has owned other, newer Corvettes, but he still prefers the '62 as a "balance" between the "classic" sports car of old and the handling and power of later models.

Despite four previous owners and 27 years, the Corvette's Ermine White lacquer finish and black vinyl interior are still original and sparkle like new. The car's VIN and engine numbers match, and the carburetor, distributor and generator numbers are also correct. Except for the battery and tires, this '62 is about as pristine a Corvette as one could find.

large and unmaneuverable by traditional sports car enthusiasts, while the Powerglide automatic was thought too much of a sell-out to Detroit marketing tastes. Meanwhile, the buying public, while taken with the new styling, did not respond in the numbers GM had projected. Many were unimpressed with the cramped interior and lack of good foul-weather protection.

With even poorer sales of '55 models, despite a new V-8 option, there was a time when it seemed the Corvette might not survive. But plans were in the works for a more handsome redesign and substantial improvements in 1956-57 models, including a standard V-8, optional four-speed, and roll-up windows, among other changes.

Still unprofitable, this was a time for Corvette to prove its mettle. Along with major '56 revisions came both factory and non-factory encouragement of Corvette as a track competitor. Corvette's performance was impressive,

Above: driveReport 'Vette carries factory original Guide T-3 headlamps. *Below and right:* Familiar crossed flags theme is found front and back.

How To Decipher Corvette Numbers

An original, unrestored Corvette in good condition is among the most prized of special interest autos today. Probably the most important requirement, other than condition, of an original car is that the production numbers match — that the engine and components are original. For example, our feature Corvette's VIN number is 20867S11081. The car can be identified as the 10,081st Corvette produced in 1962 out of 14,531. The engine number likewise is 211081F0412RE and can be deciphered as follows:

2	110081	F	04	12	RE
1962	10,081 units produced	Flint, MI assembly	April 12th manufacture date		340 bhp manual trans

The 1962 Corvette had a manufacturer's suggested base price of $4,038. Our feature car had a total suggested price when new of $5,116.60. This included the following options:

RPO 396, 340 bhp, 327 c.i.d. V-8	$107.60
Four-speed transmission	$188.30
Positraction 4.11:1	$43.05
Heavy duty suspension and brakes	$333.60
Detachable hardtop	$236.75
AM Wonderbar radio and antenna	$137.75
Nylon whitewall tires	$31.55
Total Option Price	$1,078.60

The 1962, when new, was not inexpensive. But considering the fact that as of this writing, an excellent original '62 can command in excess of $30,000, who says one cannot keep up with inflation?

with a '57 fuel-injected model (see *SIA* #73) recording 14.2 seconds in the quarter mile.

1958 models were altered by making them longer, wider and heavier, with a dramatic and glitzy new cockpit. When most other cars took a nosedive in sales, the 1958 model finally put Corvette in the black. With a basic 283-c.i.d., V-8, three carbureted and two fuel-injected versions were offered, along with three transmission choices and a wide assortment of rear axle ratios.

With refinements through 1960, the Corvette could be tailored for either street use or competition. Three Corvettes were entered in the 1960 LeMans, and one finished eighth in this grueling racing event.

The Corvette was again revised for 1961 — this time with a new "ducktail" rear section mated to the '58-60 front end and cockpit, the first major change since 1958. But in Corvette annals, 1962 was perhaps the most important year since introduction of the marque. 1962 marks the point where the "classic" Corvette ends and a new era of sleeker and more sharp-edged Corvettes begins — starting with the introduction of the Sting Ray in the fall of that year.

The rest of Corvette history is well known. Redesigned 1968 and later models were even longer, heavier and more aggressive looking. By 1970, Corvette had become as much a luxury car as a sports car, with a mammoth engine and almost as many amenities as a Cadillac.

In comparison to these later models, the '62 appears less imposing. Instead of ground-swooping styling, the '62,

*Above: 1962 would be the last year for the side cove on the Corvette body. **Below:** Body shape is now over three decades old but still has plenty of visual impact.*

1953-1962 Corvette Specifications and Production

Year	Wheelbase	Length	Width	Curb weight	Price	Production
1953	102"	167"	72.2"	2,705 lb.	$3,513	315
1954	102"	167"	72.2"	2,705 lb.	$3,523	3,640
1955	102"	167"	72.2"	2,799 lb.	$2,799	674
1956	102"	168"	70.5"	2,764 lb.	$3,149	3,467
1957	102"	168"	70.5"	2,730 lb.	$3,465	6,339
1958	102"	177.2"	72.8"	2,793 lb.	$3,631	9,168
1959	102"	177.2"	72.8"	2,840 lb.	$3,875	9,670
1960	102"	177.2"	72.8"	2,840 lb.	$3,872	10,261
1961	102"	177.2"	72.8"	2,905 lb.	$3,934	10,939
1962	102"	177.2"	72.8"	2,925 lb.	$4,038	14,531

specifications

© copyright 1990, Special Interest Autos

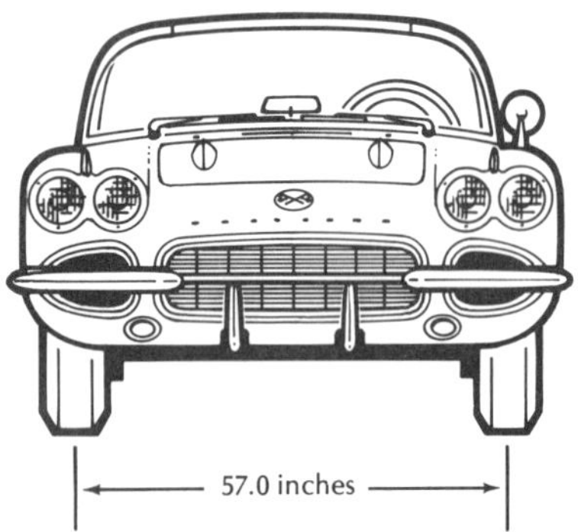

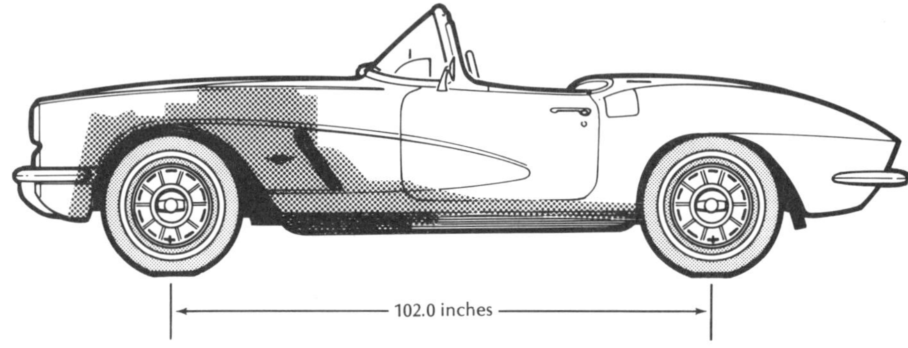

1962 Corvette

Base price new	$4,038
Standard equipment	250-bhp 327 V-8, 3-speed manual trans, heater-defroster, seat belts, electric clock, outside left rear view mirror, courtesy lights, windshield washer, dual exhaust
dR car price	$5,116 (excluding tax, lic. and destination charges)
Optional equipment on dR car	340-bhp 327 V-8, 4-speed trans, heavy duty suspension and brakes, Positraction 4.11:1 limited slip rear end, Wonderbar AM radio, detachable hardtop, whitewall tires

ENGINE

Type	Ohv V-8
Bore & stroke	4.00 inches x 3.25 inches
Displacement	327 cubic inches
Max bhp @ rpm	340 @ 6,000
Compression ratio	11.25:1
Induction system	Carter AFB 4-bbl carburetor
Exhaust system	Dual
Electrical system	12-volt, 35 amp generator

TRANSMISSION

Type	4-speed manual, fully synchronized floor mounted shift
Ratios: 1st	2.20:1
2nd	1.64:1
3rd	1.31:1
4th	1:1
Reverse	2.26:1

CLUTCH

Type	Semi-centrifugal diaphragm w/coil spring
Diameter	10 inches

DIFFERENTIAL

Type	Hypoid, semi-floating Positraction limited slip
Ratio	4.11:1

STEERING

Type	Recirculating ball, manual
Turns lock to lock	3.7
Ratio	21:1

BRAKES

Type	Hydraulic, duo-servo, self-energizing w/cast iron drums
Drum diameter	11 inches
Effective area	327 square inches

SUSPENSION

Front	Independent w/coil springs and stabilizer bar/shock absorbers
Rear	Semi-elliptic leaf springs w/ radius rods and stabilizer bar/ shock absorbers
Tires	6.70 x 15-inch ply nylon tubeless whitewall
Wheels	5 lug, steel disc

BODY & CHASSIS

Type	2-seater roadster w/folding soft top
Body construction	Fiberglass reinforced
Frame	Separate body/frame — box girder w/X member

WEIGHTS AND MEASURES

Wheelbase	102 inches
Length	177.2 inches
Width	72.8 inches
Height	52.1 inches w/hardtop (loaded) 52.2 inches w/soft top (loaded) 32.2 inches at door
Front track	57.0 inches
Rear track	59.0 inches
Road clearance	6.7 inches
Curb weight	2,925 pounds
Hardtop weight	55 pounds
Interior hip room	59.6 inches
Hat room	42.3 inches
Leg room	46.5 inches
Shoulder room	49.4 inches
Trunk room	12.1 cubic feet

CAPACITIES

Crankcase	5 qt. w/filter
Cooling system	16.5 qt. w/heater
Fuel tank	16.4 gallons

Wraparound windshields had been used on 'Vettes ever since the first series in 1953.

1962 CORVETTE

while low-slung, has the more rounded look of the original Harley Earl Corvettes. But with the first of the Sting Ray 327 V-8 engines, and with a Sting Ray-like rear deck, the '62 model was also one of the first of the new breed as well. In reality, the 1962 Corvette was a car in transition.

The unique rear treatment of the '61-62 models was inspired by Bill Mitchell's XP-700 show car of the late 1950s. The so-called "ducktail" design provided for a somewhat higher rear profile, increasing luggage space about 20 percent, with a reverse angle or tucked-in effect below the crease line featuring dual, and by now characteristically Chevrolet, round taillamps above separate horizontal bumperettes.

For the first time, the dual exhausts were positioned below the body, rather than through it or the bumpers, as in previous years. From the doors forward, with minor cosmetic refinements, the basic 1958 body shell remained. This was the styling reminiscent of the earliest Corvettes, the wraparound windshield and oval grille, the '56 coved side treatment and the longer fenders and dual headlamps added in the 1958 restyle.

By 1962, much of the brightwork, including the chrome molding around the bodyside coves, had been eliminated. The '61's chrome mesh grille was painted black, and the contrasting color insert for the coves was no longer available. There were no two-tone Corvettes in 1962. In keeping with industry trends, the optional whitewall tires were now narrow — not wide.

The cockpit was very similar to other

*Above left: Knock-off style spinners on the wheel covers were also a Corvette trademark from 1953 through 1966. **Above:** Installing or removing optional hardtop is a two-person job. **Below:** 1962 model has a little less shiny trim than previous years.*

Above: Taillamp design was carried over to the Sting Ray. **Above right:** driveReport car is equipped with optional 340-hp 327 V-8. **Below:** Center console hides clock near transmission tunnel.

1962 CORVETTE

The First and Last of Its Kind: 1962 Corvette

The 1962 Corvette is regarded by most accounts as the last and most polished of the early Corvettes. It was also an evolving car, a precursor of the more revolutionary Sting Ray yet to come. Major cosmetic changes had come in 1961, with Sting Ray-like rear styling and a new toothless grille. In many respects, however, the '62 was the first and last of its kind.

The 1962 Corvette was the:

First w/	Last w/
The 327 c.i.d. V-8 engine (base engine through '68)	The "Classic" Corvette styling
Seat belts as standard equipment	A solid rear axle
A single 4-bbl Carter carb to replace dual 4's on higher horsepower versions	A limited list of amenities (power steering, brakes, air conditioning, and leather seats offered first in '63)
An aluminum cased lighter Powerglide (optional)	The exposed headlights
Narrow style whitewall tires (optional)	An external opening conventional trunk
A heater-defroster as standard equipment	
A distributor-driven tachometer for non-fuel injected models	

third generation Corvettes. A huge, half-moon 160-mph speedometer dominated the driver's side of the dash, along with four smaller gauges for other functions and a very readable tachometer, centered right above the steering column. The passenger's side consisted of a dished-out area of the dash bridged by a horizontal grab bar and package shelf underneath. The rear-view mirror sat atop the middle of the dash, and in a console-like panel below were the electric clock and controls for the heater and optional radio. The transmission shifter and ash tray occupied the "hump" area between the seats, and located between the seat backs was the lockable glove compartment.

The seats were fairly low to the car's floor and were upholstered in a rich looking pleated vinyl, with matching door panels consisting of padded armrests, a window crank and round, white-knobbed door handle carried over from earlier models.

Mechanically, the most notable change in the '62 Corvette was the introduction of a new engine — of 327 cubic inches — essentially a bored-out 283 V-8 of earlier years. In addition to 250, 300 and 340-horsepower carbureted versions, the 327 came with an optional fuel-injected 360-horsepower setup. All engines used heavier duty bearings than the 283, and the top three engines received larger ports and a longer duration camshaft. Both the 340 and 360FI engines used solid lifter cams, and the top carbureted motors had a single four-barrel Carter AFB carburetor, rather than the twin four-

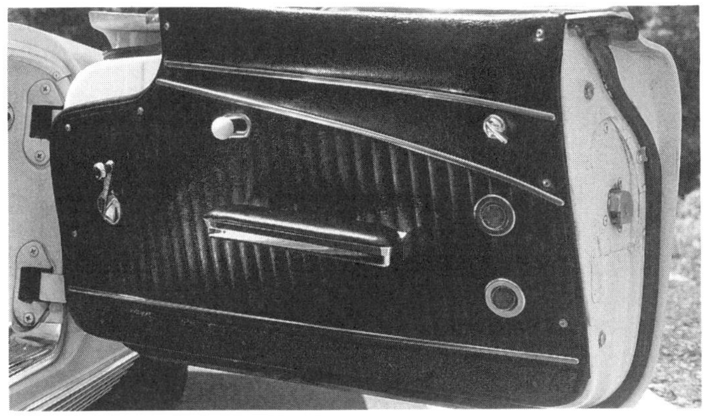 

Above: Door trim is hardly understated; top folds neatly away behind seats and under rear deck cover. *Below:* Corvette has exceptional trunk room for a two-seater thanks to sunken spare tire area. *Below:* Half-round speedo is also a familiar Corvette design component. *Bottom:* Entire interior treatment is much glitzier than 'Vette's European competition of the time.

barrel complex of previous years. The compression ratio of both the carbureted 340 and fuel-injected 360 units was 11.25:1, producing neck-snapping 0 to 60 and quarter-mile results. Other Corvette engine features included a dual point distributor and mechanical valve lifters.

A manual four-speed and Powerglide two-speed automatic were transmission options, in addition to the standard three-speed. But the Powerglide, with a new aluminum housing, was available only with the two lesser horsepower engines.

The buyer could choose sintered metallic brake linings and Positraction limited-slip differential, with a variety of different rear ends, six different ratios for the four-speed 340 and 360-horsepower models.

Unlike conventional sports cars of the time, Corvette offered a host of amenities which made motoring both sporting and comfortable. Roll-up windows had been standard since 1956. A fiberglass removable roof, in addition to a foldable soft top stored under a hatch cover flush with the body, could be bolted into place to provide quieter travel. Full instrumentation and a tachometer were standard. By 1962, Corvette provided dual-speed electric windshield wipers and washers, a heater-defroster, electric clock, dual sunvisors, cigarette lighter, parking brake warning light, courtesy lights, door safety reflectors, a lockable glove

1962 CORVETTE

box, left outside rear-view mirror, directional signals, large inside door panel arm rests, safety belts and a temperature controlled radiator fan all as standard equipment.

Truly, Corvette was not the traditional sports car of old — it was not small or Spartan in any respect. It was the American version of what Americans wanted in their sports car — a solid, fast, good looking two seater, which did not sacrifice the creature comforts to which Americans had become accustomed. More a grand touring car than a hair-shirt roadster. That's what the 'Vette delivered, in spades.   □

Bibliography
The Corvette Black Book, 1953-1988, *Michael Bruce Associates, Inc., Motorbooks International, 1988;* Corvette, America's Sports Car, *Jay Koblenz and Editors of Consumer Guide, Beekman House, 1984;* Corvette, America's Star Spangled Sports Car, The Complete History, *Karl Ludvigsen, Automobile Quarterly Pub., 1980;* Encyclopedia of American Cars, 1940-70, *Richard Langworth, Beekman House, 1980.*

Entire rear-end styling treatment is virtually identical to later Sting Ray roadsters, making the '62 a truly transitional model in design as well as engine specifications.

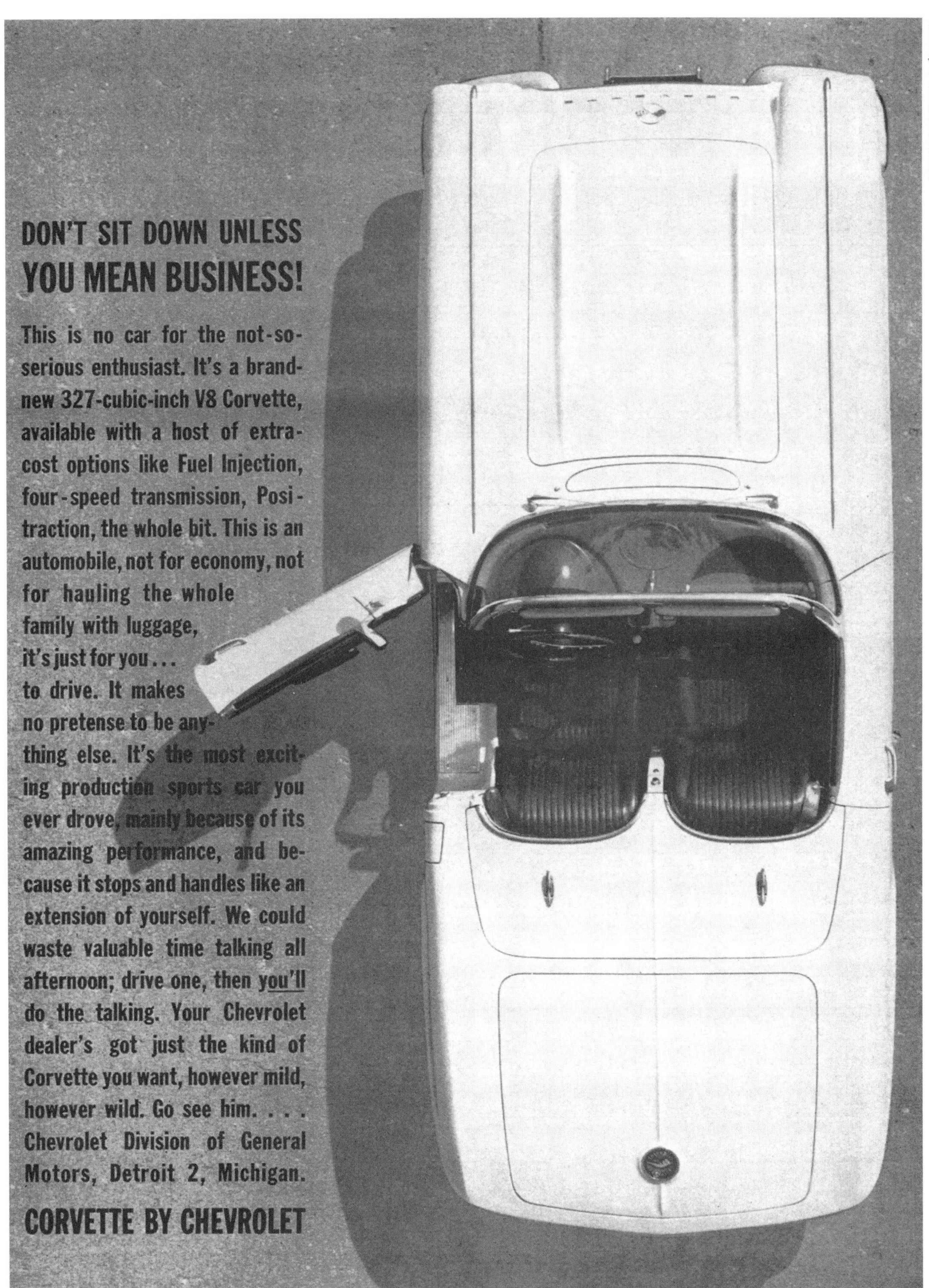

DON'T SIT DOWN UNLESS YOU MEAN BUSINESS!

This is no car for the not-so-serious enthusiast. It's a brand-new 327-cubic-inch V8 Corvette, available with a host of extra-cost options like Fuel Injection, four-speed transmission, Positraction, the whole bit. This is an automobile, not for economy, not for hauling the whole family with luggage, it's just for you . . . to drive. It makes no pretense to be anything else. It's the most exciting production sports car you ever drove, mainly because of its amazing performance, and because it stops and handles like an extension of yourself. We could waste valuable time talking all afternoon; drive one, then you'll do the talking. Your Chevrolet dealer's got just the kind of Corvette you want, however mild, however wild. Go see him. . . . Chevrolet Division of General Motors, Detroit 2, Michigan.

CORVETTE BY CHEVROLET

1963 CORVETTE STING RAY SPORT COUPE

A STYLE THAT SOARED

Originally published in Special Interest Autos #97, Jan.-Feb. 1987

by Mike Major
photos by the author

GENERAL Motors had already proved that the Corvette was here to stay. But the Corvette didn't earn much profit for Chevrolet, instead creating a lustre which enhanced its more pedestrian models.

Could not this same process be carried a step further? Corvette, of course, would never sell as much as the basic lines. But perhaps it could sell enough to become a little more profitable in its own right, and, in so doing, further highlight the image of the company as a whole. General Motors was in the contradictory position of mass producing a car supposedly uniquely personal, of making an elitist car popular, of making an impractical car appear not only as a luxury, but also as a necessary one.

The juxtaposition of these contradictions in reality is jarring. One way to resolve these contradictions is to soar above reality to the realm of dream. The selling of the '63 Corvette was the selling of a dream. For example, take a look at two of the promotions for the Sting Ray: "Only a man with a heart of stone could withstand temptation like this. You can wear a blindfold, have your wife tie you to the old family sedan, lock up the checkbook, anything of the kind; but Mister, if you ever hankered to buy a sports car, you're about to become the owner of a new Corvette Sting Ray. Sensible talk about the family budget, the good years left in your present car,

any kind of rational thought, forget it! Here's why...."

Or, "Instant Celebrity — The car you drive reflects who you are to the world. Aside from its dramatic looks and vivid performance, the new Corvette Sting Ray imparts an aura of individuality to its owner. Why? Because the Corvette Sting Ray has its own vibrant personality — but more important, because it's a uniquely different kind of car, as personal as your monogram...."

Typical advertising hype? True. Just as it's also true that virtually all advertising tries to convey this same dreamlike, unreal, so therefore very appealing mood. Everybody is trying to sell his product as the American dream. Not that many succeed, of course. However, Chevy did, with its '63 Corvette. The coupe, along with a roadster body type, both sold over 10,0000 copies, putting production for the model year over 21,500. This was about 50 percent better than any previous year. And since then the car has received ample acclaim for its landmark design.

The Sting Ray did, in fact, become America's dream car. It's interesting to see why.

First impressions don't always count. But they do here. The visual image is the embodiment of the dream, and the initial impact is that of a glacier sharpness and grace. The flowing body panels and compound-curved side windows accentuate the thrust of its aerodynamic design. Above the elegant aluminum grille, retractable headlamps rotate out of sight to meld into an unobstructed hood line. As the car sails past, the eye catches the sweep of the hood-length windsplit, the doors lifting upward into the roof, and the pleasingly subtle encasement of the rear deck.

Also adding to the overall movement of the design, and especially its dreamlike quality, is the bubble-like split rear window — a controversial feature — and the source of much contentious disagreement between chief stylist Bill Mitchell and chief engineer Zora Arkus-Duntov. Mitchell, the poet, exclaimed, "If you take that off, you might as well forget the whole thing." Duntov, on the other hand, held to the mundane view that the purpose of a rear window was to see out of. Unfortunately for Mitchell, virtually all road testers on both sides of the Atlantic responded to the practical, rather than the aesthetic aspect of the windows. Typical comments were, "...all we could see in the rear view mirror was that silly bar splitting the rear window down the middle." — *Road & Track.*

*Above: In true sports car fashion, instruments are grouped right in front of driver. **Top right:** Sting Ray designation began with '63 cars. **Above right:** driveReport car carries desirable fuel injection option. **Right:** It also has optional cast wheels. **Below:** Access to luggage compartments is from behind seats in both coupe and roadster. **Facing page:** Flip-up gas cap is placed smack in middle of fastback.*

1963 CORVETTE

"The bar down the center of the rear window makes it all but impossible to see out via the rearview mirror." — *Car Life.* "The rear window on the coupe is designed more for looks than practicality." — *Motor Trend.* The year 1963 was the first year of the Corvette's split windows. And the last.

The split window was the only glaring gaffe in the design, but it pointed out the importance of style, sometimes over convenience, which makes the split-window 'Vette so sought after today. There was no unsightly decklid, but luggage had to be squeezed over the passenger seat. There was no bulging spare tire in the back, which made both for a cleaner look and more luggage space, but it was stowed beneath the car, along with a space for tools and valuables. The steering wheel was adjustable, but not from the driver's seat. It had to be done with a wrench in the engine compartment. The foam-cushioned bucket seats were plush enough, and the seating was thoroughly comfortable, providing you were no taller than five feet, eight inches. The taller you were, the more pronounced the crick in your neck.

Form follows function. Or so the saying goes. Though in this case the opposite seems to be true. The birth of the '63 Corvette took place at Styling in the fall of '59, complete with split window. It was given the code number XP-720, and the design was substantially complete by the spring of '60. The engineers had to play catch-up, with the much more arduous task of transposing clay into steel.

This is only to say that design was the

main impetus, not that it grew in a vacuum unrelated to engineering principles, or that form and function didn't, for the most part, ultimately mesh triumphantly.

The reason for starting from scratch to come up with what would be a revolutionary design is that the other experimental models had not succeeded in pointing very clearly to the future. In December of 1957 Duntov outlined the criteria he thought should be set for the Corvette of tomorrow:

"We can attempt to arrive at the general concept of the car on the basis of our experience, and in relationship to the present Corvette. We would like to have better driver and passenger accommodation, better luggage space, better ride, better handling, and higher performance.

"Superficially, it would seem that the comfort requirements indicate a larger car than the present Corvette. However, this is not so. With a new chassis concept and thoughtful body engineering and styling, the car may be bigger internally and externally somewhat smaller than the present Corvette. Consideration of cost spells the use of a large number of passenger car components which indicates that the chassis cannot become so small that they cannot be used. I feel that considerations of ride, handling and stability dictate a frame-mounted differential."

It was this new chassis concept that matched stylish new body. The all-new independent rear suspension system, along with a shorter 98-inch wheelbase, accounted for the car's precise handling and maneuverability, and firm, level ride. *Motor Trend* called the new suspension system "far in advance, both in ride and handling, of anything now being built in the United States.... At high cruising speeds — and even at maximum speeds — nothing but an all-out competition car will equal it in stability."

The Corvette's weight was now distributed in a different way, with more than half of it now resting on the rear wheels — another first among American front-engine cars. This meant harequick handling when turning and cornering, as well as better traction on rough roads.

The '63 Corvette had nearly twice as much steel support incorporated into its central body structure compared to previous models. But this was compensated for by a reduction in fiberglass. Along with the wheelbase being shortened from 102 to 98 inches, the rear track was now two inches narrower and the frontal area was reduced by a square foot. The Sting Ray actually weighed a little less than the '62. This was a disappointment to Duntov, who had hoped for a substantial weight loss.

"However," he added, "it must be realized that several additions were made to the vehicle."

These included the thicker, more durable walls for the exhaust system, the new retractable headlights, a 20-gallon rather than 16-gallon tank, bigger brakes and more torsional strength. All important additions.

The words *Sting Ray* evoke the underwater creature that, with a flick of its tail, can release a sudden jolt of power, but generally moves with a seemingly effortless ease. The analogy fits the car, which can be cruising at 100 mph within just a few seconds (theoretical top speed of 140-142 mph) yet feels like most other cars do at 50 mph, because of the wind and engine noise minimized by the design. Yet this design evolved less from undersea considerations than airborne ones.

Though form may have initially preceded function, that form was ultimately subjected to a grueling aerodynamic testing program.

These tests were carried out at Cal Tech to measure several different coefficients including drag, lift and side forces as well as pressures and flow patterns. The purpose was to modify the design so that it could compensate for aerodynamic drag. At 60 mph, rolling resistance and aerodynamic drag are about equal. But with each mph above that the power needed to overcome aerodynamic drag increases substantially. So, under these conditions, overall performance, fuel economy, and stability are directly related to the automobile's aerodynamic shape.

Wind tunnel velocities of up to 160 mph pummeled the overall surfaces of the test models as well as about 250 tiny orifices only 27 thousandths of an inch in diameter, spaced 1-1¼ inches apart over the body surface. Visual flow observations were made from small silk tufts attached to the body as well as small dots of liquid dye. Individual runs were made not only at different speeds but also at various model angles, such as nose up, nose down, and turning positions. Virtually every attitude a car might assume under any driving condition was evaluated. The results that best minimized aerodynamic drag were incorporated into the Sting Ray's final design.

Some of the engine improvements for the Sting Ray included a positive crankcase ventilation system, a revised cooling system circuitry which gave better heat distribution during warmup, and a more accurate vacuum-advance mechanism for the distributor. An important

specifications

© copyright 1986, Special Interest Autos

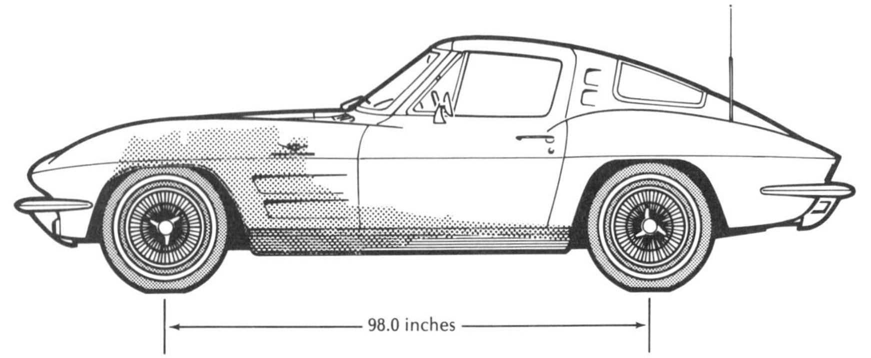

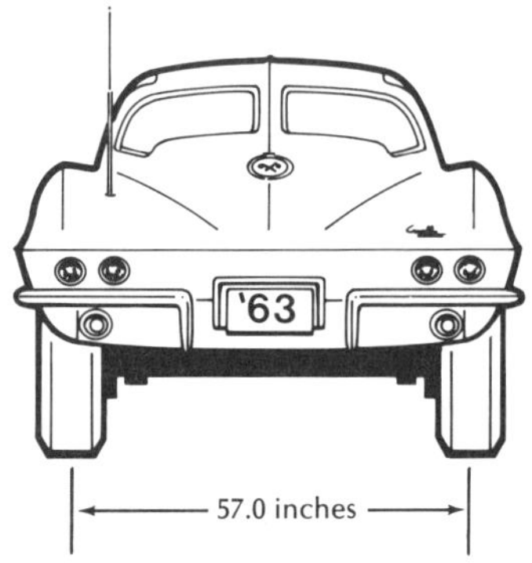

1963 Corvette Sting Ray

Price when new	$4,257 (base)
Standard equipment	Three-speed manual transmission, 250 bhp, 327 V-8 engine, AM radio
Optional equipment on dR car	Fuel injected 360 hp 327 V-8, 4-speed transmission, positraction, power steering, power brakes

ENGINE

Type	Ohv V-8
Bore & stroke	4.00 inches x 3.25 inches
Displacement	327 cubic inches
Max bhp @ rpm	360 @ 6,000
Max torque @ rpm	352 @ 4,000 rpm
Compression ratio	11.25:1
Induction system	Fuel injection
Exhaust system	Dual
Electrical system	12-volt battery/coil

CLUTCH

Type	Semi centrifugal diaphragm spring clutch
Disc diameter	10 inches
Actuation	Foot pedal

TRANSMISSION

Type	4-speed, close ratio manual, floor shift
Ratios: 1st	2.20:1
2nd	1.64:1
3rd	1.31:1
4th	1:1
Reverse	2.26:1

DIFFERENTIAL

Type	Hypoid, semi-floating (positraction)
Ratio	3.70:1

STEERING

Type	Recirculating ball
Turns, lock to lock	3.4
Ratio	17:1

BRAKES

Type	Hydraulic, duo-servo, self-adjusting w/sintered iron linings, cast-iron drums
Drum diameter	11 x 2.75" front; 11 x 2.0" rear
Total swept area	134.9 square inches

CHASSIS & BODY

Frame	Full-length, ladder-type w/5 crossmembers and separate body
Body construction	Fiberglass molded
Body style	2-passenger coupe

SUSPENSION

Front	Independent, w/coil springs, unequal length upper and lower control arms, direct-acting tubular shocks and anti-roll bar
Rear	Independent, w/fixed differential, transverse 9-leaf spring, lateral struts and universally jointed axle shafts, radius arms and direct-acting tubular shocks
Tires	6.70 x 15 4-ply nylon tubeless tires
Wheels	5-lug, steel disc

WEIGHTS AND MEASURES

Wheelbase	98.0 inches
Overall length	175.3 inches
Overall height	49.8 inches
Overall width	69.6 inches
Front track	56.3 inches
Rear track	57.0 inches
Ground clearance	5 inches
Curb weight	3,150 pounds

CAPACITIES

Crankcase	5 qts. w/filter
Cooling system	16.5 qts. w/heater
Fuel tank	20 US gallons

PERFORMANCE

Acceleration: 0-30	2.9 seconds
0-45	4.2 seconds
0-60	5.8 seconds
Standing start ¼ mi	14.5 seconds and 102 mph

(from May 1963 *Motor Trend*)

1963 CORVETTE

feature on this 360-hp engine was the Rochester fuel injection, having undergone its first major design overhaul since its introduction six years earlier. The '63 fuel injection was more precise and effective in operation, constantly adjusting itself to different humidity, temperature and altitude conditions.

The twin-cockpit dashboard, which with some variation has been with Corvette since the first '53 model, was retained. The functional instrument grouping, including speedometer, tachometer, new trip odometer, ammeter, oil pressure, fuel and temperature gauges made an impressive-looking cluster, directly in front of the driver's eyes, and the shift lever was within easy reach.

The Sting Ray was a car designed not only to be a mass-produced personalized car, an elitist car for the masses, it was also to be a production car winning on the racetrack.

As Duntov recalled, "When we came out with the Sting Ray, the car had superior handling to the previous model, and lower drag. While it was growing, I thought that this car would not only snap at Ferraris — I mean GT-type Ferraris; at that time production car racing was a popular type of racing — but this car's chassis can take increases in power as subsequent development proved. We can work on that, I felt, and we would be the very top dog, better than Ferrari in this type of competition. The calculation was made without Carroll Shelby!"

Shelby was the famous Texas road racer, co-winner of the 1959 Le Mans. Ironically, he had long wanted to build his own car and approached Chevrolet with the idea of having Scaglietti in Italy put several lightweight bodies on the Corvette chassis. Chevrolet nixed the idea, so Shelby went to Ford, who gave him the backing to build a car with an English AC chassis under a new small

Far left: 360 horse fuelie engine was a $430.40 option. **Left:** *Head room is tight for the average-sized driver.* **Below left:** *Gullwing shaped dash dips right down to console.* **Below:** *That little bit of fiberglass running down its back makes all the difference in value between the '63 and later Sting Ray coupes.*

Ford V-8 engine. This gave its 2,020-pound weight an insuperable competition advantage over the 3,150-pound Corvette. Shelby's car was called the Cobra. It beat the Corvette, badly, not only once, but time and time again. A typical public response was the *Road & Track* '63 cover story titled "Corvette vs. Cobra: The Battle for Supremacy." The article's conclusion was that "the domination of Corvette in its racing category came to an end."

A spokesman for Corvette says that the SCCA "goofed" in classifying the Cobra as a production car, since only some 900 AC-based Cobras were manufactured in all, and that it was really designed as a race car.

After his initial disappointment, Duntov was philosophical: "Fortunately, we did not suffer any to speak of. We did still win some races. But the car became recognized as a good value, good product, on its own. Even if it doesn't win the races right now, it's still the best thing you can buy. So this lack of racing success, I think, at that point did not result in a drop of sales. And a different type of people got attracted to this car. It was a vastly improved car. It had only one problem: It did not win the races against Cobra, yet Cobra did not compete with the car in the marketplace."

The Sting Ray did not have to win on a real race track. For it was a dream car. It was enough that the American everyman driving it felt it was designed solely to allow him to win his personal race against fate.

Driving Impressions

Stooping way down to get into the car is a bit awkward, and head space is cramped. But, once settled into the bouncy bucket seat, with your hands on the wide steering wheel it's comfortable enough, though not at all lulling. The feeling is as if you're behind the wheel of some space ship about to take off. And take off it does, accelerating 0 to 60 in 5.8 seconds with two people on board, about the same rate as when it was new. The owner, Bob Unger, estimates it could probably hit 135 or 140 mph. Though in this age of the 55-mile-an-hour limit, we're not about to try.

Though it takes off quickly, it has to be started cautiously. Only one pump of the accelerator, for it's easy to flood.

The driving is steady and smooth, whether on the freeway, in the city, or on rough country roads. The car seems almost to be driving itself, which is not the safest fantasy to entertain. It maneuvers easily and earns the high praise it received when it first came out for cornering well. Though, not surprisingly, the new Corvettes require even less effort.

The driveReport car is not a high-option one. It has special aluminum knock-off wheels, power brakes and AM/FM radio. But it does not have the sintered iron brake lining or power windows which would have cost, originally, $37.50 or $59.20 respectively.

The car has had only three owners: an attorney, a floorcovering merchant, and its present owners, Bob and Nancy Unger, who own the Western Corvette Supply in Bothell, Washington. Before the Ungers purchased it, it had only 70,000 miles, and was a pampered car, except for the time its front end was smashed in. It was only when Unger was painting the front end, and he found fillers he didn't like, that he decided to do a complete restoration, using all-original GM parts. The restoration took two years and is complete in virtually every respect, except that the car did not come off the frame. Unger felt it was clean enough so that the effort was not necessary. But even the clock works, which is a rarity on any postwar car.

The car is still being pampered. Unger had driven it only about five miles since the restoration and before the drive test. He feels it's too good to drive, so it sits in his garage, taking up needed space. For this reason he put it up for sale. It's a heck of a state of affairs when you have a dream car that's too good to drive and just gets in the way. ☐

Acknowledgements and Bibliography
Road & Track, Car Life, Motor Sport, Autocar, Motor Trend, Car and Driver, *and other trade and general publications, various issues;* Corvette, Sportscar of America, *Michael Bruce Associates, Inc.;* Corvette, Past-Present-Future, *Beekman House;* Corvette Automobile Quarterly, *Library Series Book; General Motors public relations and archives; and special thanks to John Paul Nelson III.*

King Kong Sting Ray

by Robert C.
Ackerson

Photos by Robert P. Hage

1967 Corvette 427

THE SIMPLE FACT IS: The Corvette is like no other automobile produced in America since World War II. If such a thing exists, it is the classic example of the special interest automobile. Looking into the Corvette's 25-year history, three events come into focus as being particularly pivotal in its evolution.

Obviously the decision of General Motors back in 1953 to commence production of the first Corvette with a fiberglass body rates foremost. It was a beginning auspicious in many respects but also one tainted with the ingredients of failure. A strange conglomeration of anachronistic features such as side curtains and a non-sporting Powerglide transmission very nearly killed the Corvette off as an infant. In effect, the early Corvette, while being a better car vis-a-vis its contemporaries than is generally recognized, tried to be too many things to too many people. In the process it became a car without a firm base of support. Thus GM, viewing any expenditure geared toward the Corvette's continuation as being a prime example of throwing good money after bad, could have, in 1955, simply dropped the whole idea. This didn't happen and American automotive history is far better for it.

Nurtured by the likes of Zora Arkus-Duntov, Ed Cole and John Fitch, it experienced a metamorphic change in 1956 and soon became an automobile possessing such unique appeal that its popularity and reputation were recognized by all elements of the motoring world. Sports car fans embraced the Corvette with only the mildest of reservations. Only the most adamant "sports cars can only be built in Europe" types refused to give it its due. The hot rodder had no such prejudices to overcome. The Corvette was homegrown, parts were easy to come by, and dollar for dollar it offered more performance than any other production car built anywhere in the world.

By the late fifties, however, the Corvette was reaching the limits of its development. The great 283-cid V-8 still offered fertile grounds for further refinement, but the same could not be said of its chassis and suspension. Similarly, its styling had taken on a definite change for the worse in 1958 with the addition of meaningless rear deck chrome stripes and non-functional hood embellishments.

These were the basic reasons behind the appearance of the Corvette Sting Ray in 1963. There were, however, several developments taking place both on the periphery and inside the corporate structure at General Motors that were to endow the Sting Ray with its own very special personality. The so-called Q-Corvette episode, for instance. In 1957 plans were afoot at General Motors for the introduction of a new passenger car that would possess such design features as a fully independent rear suspension, a rear-mounted transmission in union with the differential, and inboard-mounted rear

Originally published in Special Interest Autos #50, Mar.-Apr. 1979

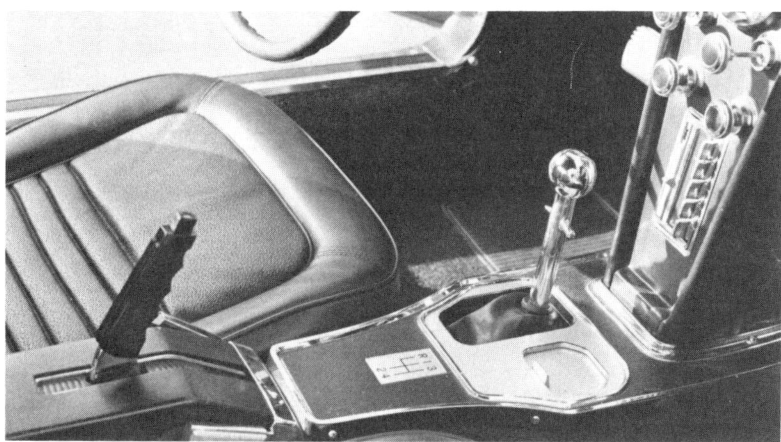

Clockwise from top left: After twelve years, Sting Ray coupe's styling still looks fresh and modern. Sting Ray's high fender bulges are balanced by crease running length of body. Full instrumentation, big round dials transmit vital info at a glance. 1967 marked first year of centrally mounted hand brake. Previous Vettes had them under dash.

brakes. Obviously a sports car version would be a natural, and for a time in 1957-58 work took place on a Corvette, scheduled for introduction in 1960, with these features incorporated into its design. A multitude of reasons involving economics and the finite limits of human resources wrote an end to this project in its original form, although the appearance of the Pontiac Tempest with its transaxle (SIA #48) was an obvious spinoff.

Of particular importance to the Corvette Sting Ray's development was the styling of the Q-Corvette. Its basic configuration was that of a fastback coupe: very low (46 in.), very sleek and very good looking.

This design, which was completed in full-size mock-up form by December 1957, was for "Corporate Eyes Only." Such was not the case, though, at Maryland's Marlboro Raceway on April 18, 1959. Making its debut before a startled and duly impressed crowd of race fans was the Sting Ray racer owned by GM Vice President in Charge of Styling, Bill Mitchell. In appearance, the Sting Ray suggested a roadster version of the Q-Corvette. The basic design was dominated by the high razor edge line that encircled the entire body and clearly divided it into upper and lower sections. In the 1940s and 1950s the trend had been to incorporate both the fenders and body of an automobile into a single form. The Q-Corvette and Sting Ray genre was a rejection of the organic design. Yet instead of returning to the old vertical delineation between elements of the automobile's structure, the appearance of the Sting Ray emphasized a horizontal division of its body surface. Above each wheel were clearance bulges similar but not identical to those appearing on the Q-Corvette. Other styling features carried over into the Sting Ray from the Q-Corvette were its low, wide grille and turtle-shell-shaped rear deck.

The impact of Mitchell's Sting Ray upon the appearance of the 1963 Corvette qualifies it for particular recognition as a design of unusual merit. When the '63 Corvette made its debut, *Corvette News* wrote that "The Sting Ray received such favorable comments from the general public that General Motors decided it was too good to pass up." Karl Ludvigsen explained its impact upon Corvette history in even more direct and succinct language in *Corvette: America's Star Spangled Sports Car.* "The motif originated for the Q-Corvette and fur-ther developed for the Sting Ray," he wrote, "had taken unshakable hold of the stylists at the Technical Center. They knew they would someday apply it to a production Corvette."

A less-than-successful and, fortunately, quickly terminated attempt to graft Sting Ray styling into the existing Corvette body shell was succeeded in late 1959 by the initiation of work on an all-new Corvette. First known as the XP-720 project, it would lead four years later to the production of the revolutionary 1963 Corvette, which in its chassis design still remains as the basis of the present day car.

Paralleling the influence of the Q-Corvette Sting Ray in the styling of the new Corvette was Zora Arkus-Duntov's impact upon its engineering. As early as 1957 he had identified four basic areas where the Corvette could be substantially upgraded. Among Duntov's priorities were better accommodations for both the driver and passenger, improved luggage space, upgraded handling and riding qualities, and a general overall improvement in the Corvette's performance.

The technical developments of the Corvette are punctuated with influences of the phantom-like, never

Illustrations by Russell von Sauers, The Graphic Automobile Studio

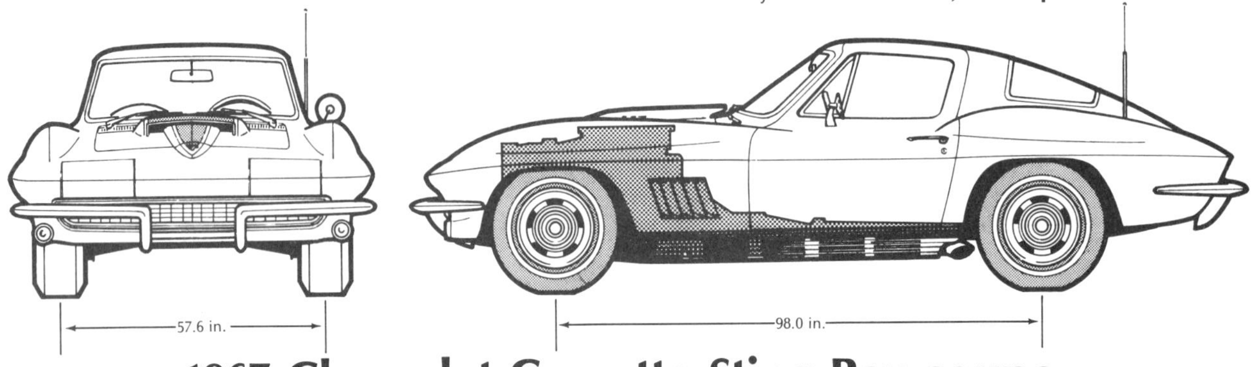

1967 Chevrolet Corvette Sting Ray coupe

Price when new	$5544.05 (base price—fob Detroit $4388.75).

Optional equipment	Positraction, $42.15; Shoulder belts, $26.35; 435 hp engine, $437.10; Soft Ray tinted glass (all windows), $15.80; Full-transistor ignition, $73.75; AM-FM radio with rear fixed height antenna, $172.75; Special Purpose front and rear suspension, $36.90; 4-speed manual close-ratio transmission, $184.35; 7-75x15 2-ply (4PR) Special Firestone Nylon red stripe tires, $46.65; Freight, $59.75.

ENGINE

Type	Ohv V-8.
Bore & Stroke	4.251 x 3.76 in.
Displacement	427.0 cid.
Maximum bhp	435 @ 5800 rpm.
Maximum torque	460 @ 4000 rpm.
Compression ratio	11.0:1.
Induction system	Triple 2-bbl carburetors with High-Flow air cleaner.
Exhaust system	Dual exhaust/mufflers.
Electrical system	12-volt coil.

TRANSMISSION

Type	4-speed, close ratio manual.

DIFFERENTIAL

Type	Positraction, frame-mounted.
Ratio	3.55:1.

STEERING

Type	Recirculating ball.
Turns lock to lock	2.9.
Ratio	17.6:1.
Turning circle	41.6 ft.

BRAKES

Type	Vented discs, 11.75 in. diameter, single calipers.
Total swept area	461 sq. in.

CHASSIS & BODY

Frame	Steel ladder.
Body construction	Fiberglass.
Body style	2-seater coupe.

SUSPENSION

Front	Independent, unequal-length A-arms, coil springs, tubular shock absorbers, anti-roll bar.
Rear	Independent, transverse leaf spring, transverse struts, half shafts with U-joints, trailing arms, tubular shock absorbers.
Tires	(original) Redwall, 7.75 x 15 2-ply nylon.
Wheels	6-inch wide, pressed steel.

WEIGHTS & MEASURES

Wheelbase	98.0 in.
Overall length	175.2 in.
Overall width	69.6 in.
Overall height	49.6 in.
Frontal area	19.2 sq. ft.
Front tread	57.6 in.
Rear tread	58.3 in.
Curb weight	3140 lbs.

CAPACITIES

Crankcase	5.0 qt.
Fuel tank	18.5 gal.

PERFORMANCE

0-60 mph	5.37 sec.
0-100 mph	11.8 sec.
Top speed	156 mph

1967 Production 22,940; coupes—8504, convertibles 14,436.

1967 Corvette

All Sting Ray coupes from 1964 through '67 had one-piece rear window.

produced but always lurking the background rear-engine Corvette. This period of time was no exception. Two proposals, one with a Corvair engine, the other with conventional V-8 power and using suspension elements from the Q-sedans, existed, but since they were susceptible to serious technical, economic and design criticisms, they were abandoned. Yet their legacy was seen in the Sting Ray's 47%-53% front-rear weight distribution. Duntov had entertained the hope that the new Corvette would be considerably lighter than the model it replaced. Carroll Shelby's famous statement, that if a driver could handle "that Hawg" (read Corvette) he could handle anything,

pinpointed an area where the Corvette could stand improvement.

In their road-ready form there was little difference between the 1962 and 1963 Corvettes. The older model weighed in at approximately 3080 pounds, the Sting Ray was only some fifty pounds lighter. Yet this weight similarity was deceptive.

The real key to improving the roadability of the Corvette was not merely the lowering of the overall weight. Equally important was the reduction of its unsprung weight. Simply put, the greater the ratio of the sprung weight (that of all components supported by the springs) to unsprung weight (that which moves up and down with the wheels), the better both the ride and handling of an automobile becomes. Tire adhesion, especially on rough roads, improves and the driver and passenger become less conscious of the vertical movement of the wheels. The 1963 Corvette was in this category far superior to its predecessors.

The front suspension of the Sting Ray was very conventional, consisting of components used on the large Chevrolet sedans. As Duntov told the Society of Automotive Engineers, the front suspension elements of the Chevrolet sedan were "just rearranged" on the Corvette. The results, a conventional coil spring and unequal length wishbone arrangement did its job in more than one sense. Not only was it a competent set-up, but since it used parts already developed, tested and in production, it represented a substantial savings over the expense of providing the Corvette with its own all-new front suspension. Thus the low cost of the Corvette's front suspension helped Duntov justify the cost of the independent rear suspension he deeply desired for the Corvette.

While the use of a nine leaf transverse spring at the rear would seem retrogressive, it was only on the most superficial grounds that the Corvette's independent rear suspension could be called old fashioned. With the exception of the leaf spring (some '63 prototypes were tested with rear coil springs but economics ruled out their use on production models), the basic layout of the Sting Ray rear suspension was derived from the CERV-1 research vehicle. Radius arms controlled the fore and aft movement of the rear wheels as well as absorbing driving and braking reaction forces. Lateral control was provided by two control rods and the axle shaft. A major contributing factor in the reduction of unsprung weight at the rear was the mounting of the differential directly to the frame. Total rear unsprung weight dropped from 301 pounds on 1962 Vettes to only 200 pounds on the Sting Ray.

A problem typical of most independent rear suspension systems, the tendency of the rear tires to develop a strong positive camber when turns were taken at high speeds, was obviously unacceptable in a car of the Corvette's caliber. By building 1.5 degrees of negative camber into the rear wheels when they were normally loaded, the Corvette engineers eliminated this problem.

From a mechanical point of view, the only items carried over from 1962 were the four-speed transmission and the 327-cid V-8. The base engine for the Sting Ray with a compression ratio of 10.5:1 and hydraulic lifters was rated at 250 hp. The use of a larger, aluminum-bodied carburetor pushed the horsepower to 300. The Ramjet fuel-injected V-8 with the Mark I Duntov cam, solid lifters and 11.25:1 compression ratio weighed in at 360 hp. Of a design basically identical to that used on earlier Corvettes, the fuel

He Directed the Show

There probably isn't an SIA reader who didn't while away a dull study hall or quiet evening drawing pictures of cars. It's a natural affliction of the car hobby and most of us can admit to sketching out our version of the ultimate dream car. This propensity towards doodling gives us all one thing in common with William Mitchell, former GM Vice President of Design, currently a design consultant, and beyond question the dominant force in the styling of postwar American automobiles.

Mitchell still possesses the scrapbook containing the automobile drawings he did as an eight year old. Young Mitchell's enthrallment with the automobile was certainly aided by the occupation of his father, a Buick dealer who took in trade such delights as Stutz Bearcats, various Mercedes et al, none of which escaped the once-over by young Mitchell.

Yet, working with his father in his Greenville, Pennsylvania, dealership was not what Mitchell wanted. Instead, in 1927 he found employment at the Barron Collier advertising agency in New York City as an office boy. This in turn led to a full-time job after his graduation from high school. Mitchell's work as a layout man and illustrator was not particularly unusual, but it did bring him into contact with the three sons of Barron Collier, who like Mitchell, were totally infatuated with automobiles. As teenagers, Barron Collier Jr, and his two younger brothers, Sam and Miles, raced the 1930s equivalent of Go-Karts on the roads of "Overlook," their parents' estate located at Pocantico Hills, New York. This type of spirited, if low key and primitive, form of motor sport led in 1933 to the creation of the Automobile Racing Club of America, which in the words of John C. Rueter, the author of the ARCA's definitive history, *American Road Racing*, "probably had as many letters in its full title as it had members."

During the 1930s the ARCA grew in stature and, if not in quantity of members, certainly in the quality of the races it sponsored. Today's Sports Car Club of America not only is its modern day counterpart but has the very roots of its existence in the activities of the Automobile Racing Club of America.

For William Mitchell the ARCA also was part of his blossoming affair with the automobile. On July 14, 1934, the ARCA sponsored a "Prix d'Endurance" race on a 0.7 mile course dubbed the Sleepy Hollow Ring which the Colliers had created at Pocantico Hills. Again, quoting Rueter, "One of the interested spectators at this memorable event, which was run in daylight and half in darkness, was William E. Mitchell...."

Shortly thereafter Mitchell hung some of his sketches of that event on the walls of his office where they naturally attracted the attention of the Collier boys. Mitchell was then enlisted by them to design an emblem for the ARCA, an assignment he was happy to undertake. The result of his efforts was as classic as the cars then being raced by the ARCA. It featured a head-on view of an Auburn Speedster, stars and stripes, and the club's name. Mitchell also designed one of the first MG ads for Motor Sport, Inc., a firm established by Sam and Miles Collier to sell MGs in America. But there was another far more important result of Mitchell's ARCA sketches. Walter Carey, an ad agency executive who attended at least one ARCA event, saw them as the products of a talent better put toward the designing of cars than the designing of ads for them. Since Carey was also a personal friend of Harley Earl, his suggestion that Mitchell send Earl some examples of his work was not something to be lightly dismissed. Mitchell did as Carey advised and on December 15, 1935, William Mitchell joined General Motors.

Mitchell's first major success at Earl's Art and Colour kingdom was the Cadillac Sixty Special. Although Mitchell looks back at that project as something that was not the type of car he really wanted to design, it does, because of its singularity, represent one of the Corvette's ancestors from the Classic Age.

When Mitchell succeeded Earl as Vice President in charge of the GM Design Staff on December 1, 1958, the Corvette had already passed from infancy into adolescence. Those were not exactly years of glory for GM styling and their 1959 cars were even more garish and excessive than the '58s. But since the gap from styling prototype to production model is a span of a thousand days, there was little Mitchell could do to immediately demonstrate the change in command. In the case of the Corvette, however, there was an interesting option: the creation of a one-off special that would mark the beginning of Mitchell's reign. Using the chassis of the old SS "Mule" that had been the practice car at Sebring in 1957, Mitchell had stylist Larry Shinoda create the first Sting Ray, which served in effect as the prototype of the 1963 production model Sting Ray. In spirit if not form, the Sting Ray, which raced in SCCA competition in 1959 and 1960 before being refurbished as a show car, was the modern counterpart of the MGs, Bugattis and Amilcars that had raced years earlier around the Sleepy Hollow Ring. Certainly it was appropriate that an ARCA emblem was mounted in the Sting Ray's cockpit.

Mitchell's hand could not be behind every stroke of the pen that designed the '63 Sting Ray. Yet it is clear that, without Mitchell at the helm of GM styling, things might have been very, very different. Mitchell said it best in *Corvette: A Piece of the Action:* "Michelangelo didn't paint the whole Sistine Chapel by himself, he had a lot of help, but he was directing the show." It was a very good show that Mitchell directed. □

From Z06 to L-88:
A Stampede of Horses

Throughout the five years of its existence, the first series Sting Ray was available with a long list of competition items. While they were never quite able to turn the tide in racing against the Shelby Cobras, these goodies nonetheless made the Corvette a formidable performer.

The basic competition Z06 racing option for 1963 was initially available only for the Sting Ray coupe. The core of this option was the 327 cubic inch, 360 hp Ramjet fuel-injected V-8 connected to Chevrolet's nearly flawless four-speed transmission and Positraction limited-slip differential. Other important components of the Z06 package included a heavy-duty power brake system, finned cast-iron drums with sintered metallic linings, vented backing plates and air scoops.

The suspension was also given its share of attention, receiving a heavy-duty front stabilizer bar and considerably stiffer front and rear springs as well as stronger shock absorbers all around. Special cast aluminum 3-lug knock-off wheels and a 36 gallon fuel tank were also included in the Z06's $1818.45 price. Chevrolet later gave in to customer demands that the Z06 option also be made available for the convertible Sting Ray. However, in doing so, the 36 gallon tank and aluminum wheels became separate items with the former still installable only in the coupe.

The 360 hp Corvette was a capable performer; a zero to 60 mph time of 5.6 seconds was not an unusual accomplishment for a Z06 Corvette. Top speed of course was highly dependent upon a given car's rear axle ratio. On GM's five mile banked track at Milford, Michigan, a 360 hp coupe with a 3.08:1 rear axle and oversize 8.20x15 tires was timed at 161 mph. A convertible with the same setup was five mph slower.

Since peak horsepower was, at 375 hp, only marginally greater in 1964, there was relatively little difference in straight line performance between the 1963 and 1964 Sting Rays. Of historical interest was the replacement of the almost legendary Duntov Mark I cam of 1956 vintage with a new high lift job in both the 375 hp fuel-injected V-8 and its high-performance running mate, a Holley 4150 4-barrel carburetor-equipped engine rated at 365 hp.

The Corvette never fit into the European concept of a small-displacement, high-output-engined sports car, but after March 1965 it became a leviathan among sports cars with the availability of the 396 cid, 425 hp Turbo-Jet or Mark IV V-8. Corporate policy at that time decreed that no division could offer any of their intermediate-sized models with engines of more than 400 cubic inches. Thus the Mark IV was a scaled-down version of the 427 cid Chevrolet V-8 first raced in the 1963 Daytona 500. While it did not emerge the winner, it shook the Ford camp by qualifying two mph faster than anyone else. The Mark IV was rated very conservatively at 425 hp. With this new source of power available (zero to 100 mph consumed only 13 seconds), the 375 hp fuel-injection option became rather meaningless.

Logically, the following year when the Mark IV grew to 427 cubic inches, the fuel-injected engine was no longer offered. The "ha-ha" 425 hp rating was carried over for 1966, but judging from its performance, a true figure would not fall far short of 500. Similar hokum continued in 1967 when the Mark IV with triple Holley two-barrel carburetors was modestly endowed with an official 435 hp at 5800 rpm rating.

"Proceed with caution" was *Corvette News'* advice as it introduced its readers to the ultimate regular performance option for the 1963-67 Sting Rays, the L-88. *Corvette News* went on to describe the L-88 as "not an engine for ordinary everyday driving. It gives a rough idle, is not the easiest engine to start, and was not designed with high fuel economy in mind. As a matter of fact the L-88 requires higher octane gas than most stations carry. It is strictly a high-performance engine for competition use." Among the features that set the L-88 apart from the L-71 435 hp, 427 cid V-8 were its lightweight aluminum heads, 12.5:1 compression ratio, larger exhaust valves and even higher lift cam. Karl Ludvigsen credited the L-88 with "a reliably reported power figure" of 560 hp at 6500 rpm running on the minimum recommended fuel with a 103 research octane rating.

The L-88 engine option listed for $1500, but this was just the first raid on the would-be purchaser's bank account since along with the L-88 came a long list of mandatory options. These included heavy-duty power disc brakes ($342.30), heavy-duty front and rear suspension ($36.90), a fully transistorized ignition ($73.75) and the M22 "bone-crusher" transmission. Deletion of the heater-defroster unit was required in order to (in the words of *Corvette News*) "cut down on weight and discourage the car's use on the street."

A total of only 20 L-88-powered Corvettes were built in 1967, of which just 16 were equipped with the aluminum heads. Before it blew up, an L-88 Corvette was clocked at 171.5 mph down the Mulsanne straight during the 1967 LeMans race. Chevrolet test drivers pushed an L-88 to 183 mph on the GM test track at Milford, Michigan.

Corvette Engine Guide   1963–1967

	Displacement (cubic inches)	Horsepower	Compression ratio	Torque (ft. lb.)	Cam, lifters	Induction System
1963	327 Base	250 at 4400 rpm	10.5:1	350 at 2800 rpm	standard cam, hydraulic lifters	one-4-barrel Carter WCFB carburetor
	327 (RPO L-75)	300 at 5000 rpm	10.5:1	360 at 3200 rpm	standard cam, hydraulic lifters	one-4-barrel aluminum Carter AFB carburetor
	327 (RPO L-76)	340 at 6000 rpm	11.25:1	344 at 4000 rpm	Duntov cam, mechanical lifters	one-4-barrel aluminum Carter AFB carburetor
	327 (RPO L-84)	360 at 6000 rpm	11.25:1	352 at 4000 rpm	Duntov cam, mechanical lifters	Ramjet fuel injection
1964	327 Base	250 at 4400 rpm	10.5:1	350 at 2800 rpm	standard cam, hydraulic lifters	one-4-barrel Carter WCFB carburetor
	327 (RPO L-75)	300 at 5000 rpm	10.5:1	360 at 3200 rpm	standard cam, hydraulic lifters	one-4-barrel aluminum Carter AFB carburetor
	327 (RPO L-76)	365 at 6200 rpm	11.0:1	350 at 4000 rpm	high lift cam, mechanical lifters	one-4-barrel Holley 4150 carburetor
	327 (RPO L-84)	375 at 6200 rpm	11.0:1	350 at 4400 rpm	high lift cam, mechanical lifters	Ramjet fuel injection
1965	327 Base	250 at 4400 rpm	10.5:1	350 at 2800 rpm	standard cam, hydraulic lifters	one-4-barrel WCFB carburetor
	327 (RPO L-75)	300 at 5000 rpm	10.5:1	360 at 3200 rpm	standard cam, hydraulic lifters	one-4-barrel Carter AFB carburetor
	327 (RPO L-79)	350 at 5800 rpm	11.0:1	360 at 3600 rpm	high lift (0.447 inch) cam, hydraulic lifters	one-4-barrel Holley 4150 carburetor
	327 (RPO L-76)	365 at 6200 rpm	11.0:1	350 at 4000 rpm	high lift cam, mechanical lifters	one-4-barrel Holley 4150 carburetor
	327 (RPO L-84)	375 at 6200 rpm	11.0:1	350 at 4400 rpm	high lift cam, mechanical lifters	Ramjet fuel injection
1965 ½	396 (RPO L-78)	425 at 6400 rpm	11.0:1	415 at 4000 rpm	high lift cam, mechanical lifters	one-large 4-barrel Holley carburetor
1966	327 Base	300 at 5000 rpm	10.5:1	350 at 2800 rpm	standard cam, hydraulic lifters	4-barrel Holley
	327 (L79)	350 at 5800 rpm	11.0:1	360 at 3000 rpm	high performance cam, hydraulic lifters	4-barrel Holley
	427 (L-30)	390 at 5200 rpm	10.25:1	460 at 3600 rpm	high performance, hydraulic lifters	4-barrel Holley
	427 (L-72)	425 at 5000 rpm	11.0:1	460 at 4000 rpm	special performance cam, mechanical lifters	large 4-barrel Holley
1967	327 base	300 at 5000 rpm	10.0:1	360 at 3400 rpm	standard cam, hydraulic lifters	4-barrel Holley
	327 (RPO L-79)	350 at 5800 rpm	11.0:1	360 at 3600 rpm	high performance cam, hydraulic lifters	4-barrel Holley
	427 (RPO L-36)	390 at 5400 rpm	10.25:1	460 at 3600 rpm	high performance cam, hydraulic lifters	4-barrel Holley
	427 (RPO L-71)	435 at 5800 rpm	11.0:1	460 at 4000 rpm	special performance cam, mechanical lifters	three Holley two-barrels
	421 (RPO L-89)*	435 at 5800 rpm	11.0:1	460 at 4000 rpm		
1967 ½	427 (L-88)	560 at 6400 rpm	12.5:1		ultra high (.5365" intake) cam	1-Holley 850CFM carburetor

The L-89 option was in effect the L-71 engine with aluminum heads with larger exhaust valves and superior heat dissipation qualities.

1967 Corvette

injection system for 1963 was redesigned via a larger capacity intake manifold, larger reshaped induction ram tubes, a horizontally mounted throttle plate shaft, and a manifold heat (rather than electrically) activated automatic choke. The primary intention of these changes was to improve the Ramjet's volumetric efficiency and idling characteristics. The same engine with the large 4-barrel carburetor was rated at 340 hp.

The visual impression that the Sting Ray body possessed superior aerodynamic characteristics to its predecessor was confirmed in tests conducted at the California Institute of Technology's wind tunnel. The results of experiments with a 3/8-scale model Sting Ray coupe indicated it not only had less wind drag than a 1962 Corvette with its removable hardtop installed but that it also had a lower drag coefficient than Bill Mitchell's competition model Sting Ray. Later, on the five-mile high-speed circular track at General Motors' Milford, Michigan, proving grounds, a Sting Ray coupe attained a speed of 161 mph. This speed was reached with the Corvette running open exhausts, oversize 8.20 x 15 tires and a 3.08:1 rear axle. Similar tests with a convertible netted a maximum speed of 156 mph.

Development of the new Corvette was not without the inevitable corporate in-fighting. One contest pitted Zora Arkus-Duntov against Bill Mitchell. Both men were Corvette advocates of the highest order, but each approached the Corvette from somewhat differing points of view. Their dispute involved that feature of the 1963 Sting Ray coupes that sets them dramatically apart from other Corvettes of the 1963-67 era, their split rear window. To Duntov it was pure nonsense. It obscured vision to the rear and served no function. Mitchell literally viewed things differently. He campaigned for its retention and his opinion prevailed over Duntov's for one year. But once Mitchell peered out at the world via the rear view mirror of a '63 Sting Ray coupe, he saw the light, or lack of it. The following year the coupe had a one piece rear window.

Another proposal bounced around at this time was the idea from Chevrolet General Manager Ed Cole that a four-seater Corvette be considered. The trio of Duntov, Mitchell and *Corvette News* editor Joe Pike successfully argued against this idea. A Thunderbird-like fate for the Corvette was, from their point of view, something to be avoided at all costs.

The sports car world which had, two years earlier, been suitably impressed

by the introduction of the Jaguar XK-E (also with independent rear suspension, stunning good looks and very fast), in general received the new Corvette with open arms. "Compared with previous Corvettes," noted *Car and Driver*, "the Sting Ray is improved in almost every imaginable respect." *Sports Car Graphic*, perhaps unfairly depreciating the pre-1963 Corvette, crowed "The Corvette really comes of age as a luxury, high performance sports car." Although *Road & Track* liked the Sting Ray very much, it was, as Shelby's Cobra efforts began, somewhat inaccurate in its prophesy that "As a purely sporting car, the new Corvette will know few peers on road or track. It has proved, in its 'stone-age form,' the master of most production-line competitors; in its nice, shiny new

427 engine is conservatively rated at 435 hp. Actual horses are probably closer to 475.

Top: *Factory mirror carries Chevy bow tie imprint.* ***Bottom:*** *The view most drivers are left with when they decide to indulge in an impromptu stoplight grand prix against a 427.*

1967 Corvette

concept it ought to be nearly unbeatable."

One of the more provocative and critical road tests of the Corvette came from the pages of *The Autocar*. Calling the Sting Ray "a curious mixture of American and European concepts of what a genuine gran turismo car should be," *The Autocar* found numerous features of the Corvette not exactly to its liking. The Corvette's outstanding acceleration (in British hands, zero to 60 mph with a 360 hp coupe required 6.5 seconds) was given its due, but *The Autocar* saw the Corvette in its "refinement; particularly in respect of engine and transmission noise (as) inferior to that of most of its European competitors." This, its testers felt, gave the impression of the car "being more powerful than it really is."

In sharp contrast to *The Autocar*'s less than unbounded enthusiasm for the Corvette, *Car and Driver* praised the Corvette as a "fine showpiece of the American automobile industry, especially since it is produced at a substantially lower price than any foreign sports or GT car of comparable performance." Perhaps the ultimate antithesis to *The Autocar*'s editorial outlook at that time was *Hot Rod* magazine whose Ray Brock regarded the Sting Ray as one of the "best handling production sports cars in the world.... This car is sensational in every way" was Brock's overall reaction.

In terms of styling, performance and technical sophistication the first Sting Rays showed steady improvement each year of their production life. In 1964 came the removal both of the virtually universally disliked divided rear window and the false hood grilles that had also been a source of legitimate criticism concerning the Corvette's appearance. An interesting attempt at improving the Corvette's interior ventilation involved the installation of a fan in the side panel behind the driver's seat. A pull-type switch located on the dash near the retractable headlight control operated this fan which drew air from the cockpit out through the left roof vent. The vent in the opposite side of the car was nonfunctional. The fan was operative only when the heater was not in use. In practice this system was relatively ineffectual and was dropped after 1965.

In addition to receiving the usual power boost (sidebar page 66) and styling refinements, the 1965 Sting Ray was noted for its outstanding four-wheel disc brake system. For a short period of time the old drum brake system was offered as a "credit option," but the superiority of the disc system made this an alternative of no appeal whatsoever.

The early 1965 introduction of the Mark IV, 396-c.i.d. V-8, conservatively rated at 425-horsepower, signalled the end of one era and the start of another in terms of Corvette performance. The availability of such an engine made the continuation of the fuel-injected 375-horsepower option rather redundant. Thus, after 1966, the fuel-injected Corvette became a thing of the past. The Mark IV was expanded to 427 cubic inches in 1966 and in 1967, with three two-barrel carbs, was obviously developing far more than its rated 435 bhp.

In its final 1967 form the first generation Sting Ray was free of most of

---

Why They Look That Way

As early as September 1955 work began at GM Styling on a Corvette body style to replace the design introduced for 1956. Inspiration came from Oldsmobile's Golden Rocket, a futuristic-appearing two-passenger coupe which was nearing completion for showing in the spring '56 GM Motorama. The plan for a coupe-only Corvette with Golden Rocket overtones was shelved in a matter of months due to the existence of higher-priority projects.

In 1957 the start of engineering work on a new "Q" passenger car with independent rear suspension and transaxle once again had the rumor mill grinding out reports that a radically-styled Corvette with similar underpinning was on its way from Chevrolet.

There was substantial strength behind such speculations, for at that time stylist Bob McLean was indeed overseeing the design of a new and very advanced-looking Corvette body. The Q-Corvette existed in full-scale mock-up form by early December 1957. With a wheelbase of 98 inches and an overall height of 46 inches, the Q-Corvette, like the Sting Ray, featured hidden headlights, although on the Q-Corvette they stowed away in its forward hood section. In profile the Q-Corvette's appearance was far different than that of the then-current 1958 Corvette.

Above each wheel well was a pronounced bulge in the fender line. These would have given the Corvette a top-heavy, high-off-the-ground appearance if not for the strong horizontal crease line running the length of the body just above the wheel cutouts.

Predicting the contemporary Corvette's removable roof panels was the Q-Corvette's built-in arch behind its cockpit which, along with the rear edge of its windshield, served as the end point for a removable roof section. Economics, both of the too-expensive-to-build and "You Auto Buy Now" variety, scuttled both the Q-sedan and its Q-Corvette derivative during 1958.

But in December 1958 William Mitchell began his tenure as GM's styling boss. More than once his predecessor, Harley Earl, had moved General Motors' management mountain over to his view of how things should be by creating in full-size form whatever styling scheme he wanted GM to approve. Armed with this knowledge and imbued with a strong passion for sports cars, Mitchell resurrected two lively skeletons from the GM closet. One was the mule chassis left over from the SS racing Corvette project of 1956-57. The second was the styling of the Q-Corvette which Larry Shinoda had little difficulty working into roadster form. The result was Mitchell's road-racing Sting Ray which drivers such as Dick Thompson and John Fitch raced in SCCA competition in 1958 and 1959. This vehicle, while it bore no identification linking it either to the Corvette or Chevrolet, was viewed by the motoring press as nothing less than the leading edge of a new generation of Corvettes. This time there was to be no derailing of Corvette's future styling. The Q-Corvette-cum-Sting Ray appearance was indeed the starting point in the fall of 1959 on the design of the 1963 Corvette. By April 1960 the XP-720, as the new Corvette project was labeled, existed in a form that incorporated the coupe body format of the Q-Corvette with many detail features found on Mitchell's racing Sting Ray. It was not until after work had been completed on the Sting Ray coupe that activity commenced on its convertible running mate. This apparent reluctance on the part of the Corvette's designers to create an open Sting Ray reflects the lingering influence of the Mercedes-Benz 300SL. Yet it's worth noting that the convertible versions of both these marques were the better sellers.

When the Sting Ray was first produced in 1963 its obvious European competitor was the Jaguar E-type. As expected, the British press preferred the styling of the Jaguar to that of the Corvette. For example, *Motor Sport* observed, "It (the Sting Ray) is as vulgar and over-ornamented as the E-type is simple and functional." But while the E-type remained on the scene for too long and became hopelessly burdened with makeshift tack-ons to bring it into conformity with federal safety regulations, the first Sting Rays showed steady improvement from year to year. They surely deserved a longer production life, but, in a sense because they avoided the consequences of the heavy hand of the government upon their appearance, they remain cars that are today as youthful and fresh as the day they first dazzled the motoring world.

Corvette's Patron Saint

Zora Arkus-Duntov arrived at General Motors at virtually the same time the sports car was beginning to catch the imagination of the American motorist. General Motors was ready to launch the first production batch of 1953 Corvettes. Duntov, while not initially responsible for the refinement of the Corvette, was soon behind the wheel of the first Corvette engineering prototype sorting out its handling problems.

From that point on until his retirement in early 1975, Duntov was guiding light, advocate and patron saint of the Corvette. Unswerving in his determination to make the Corvette an even more potent sports car, he fought every corporate move that threatened to dilute its sporting blood. He didn't win every struggle but his batting average was far above .500, and, when it came to opposing such ideas as a four-seater Corvette, it was Duntov and Bill Mitchell who saw to it that such heresy was quickly snuffed out.

Duntov first came to the United States in late 1940, a 31-year-old Russian citizen who had, among other things, designed machine tools and diesel locomotive engines. In the 1930s Duntov had also developed considerable expertise both as a racing car mechanic and driver. The Second World War put an end to such activity and in 1939 Duntov, along with his brother, enlisted in the French military forces. After serving as the tail gunner on a French bomber, Duntov was released from duty after France had been defeated by Germany. His subsequent arrival in the United States had all the trappings of international political intrigue. His technical proficiency was such that certain officials preferred him to reside in America, well out of the grasp of the Nazis.

Arriving in the United States in December 1940, Duntov allowed only a small amount of time to pass before putting his talents to work (Duntov's engineering degree thesis, which was published in 1934, dealt with supercharging). Successfully designing a polyharmonic damper for several major U.S. aviation firms led to Duntov quickly becoming a consulting engineer with many prominent industrial clients.

By 1942, Duntov, along with his cousin and brother, had organized the Ardun Mechanical Corporation which contributed to the American war effort via the manufacture of both ammunition dies and aircraft components. In 1947 Duntov introduced the famous Ardun overhead valve head for the old flathead Ford V-8. For a time Duntov returned to Europe where he worked for Sydney Allard and raced his cars. In 1954 and 1955 Duntov attained class victories at LeMans with an 1100 cc Porsche Spyder.

Duntov's racing achievements with the Corvette were no less noteworthy. In January 1956 his 150.583 mph two-way run at Daytona Beach marked the start of the Corvette's years of dominance in American sports car racing. The following year his efforts that were manifested in the appearance of the SS Corvette at the Sebring twelve hour race were cut short before they really had a chance to blossom by the AMA's anti-racing, anti-performance manifesto of June 1957. For Duntov that must have been a bitter pill to swallow since he surely had visions of Corvettes at LeMans dancing in his creative head. Duntov's last appearance in competition was at the Lime Rock track in Connecticut where he drove a Maserati 250F in a Formula Libre event.

Throughout the years Duntov had to accept other corporate decrees that eventually forced him to abandon his goal of developing a lightweight, rear-engined Corvette. As a consequence the Corvette was always a larger, heavier car than Duntov really wanted. Yet Duntov was sincere when, in regard to the 1963 Sting Ray, he said that at last there was a Corvette he would really be proud to drive in Europe.

the sources of criticism the 1963 version had possessed. Its styling was immeasurably cleaner, its disc brakes truly outstanding and its suspension still one of the best in the world.

As is commonly known, Chevrolet had planned to retire the first series Sting Ray body after the 1966 models and introduce the Mako Shark II-inspired design in 1967. Difficulties encountered both of an esthetic and technical nature forced the cancellation of the new Corvette body style till 1968. And the older design was called upon to be a stand-in for 1967.

Driving Impressions

Both a visual inspection and a short stint behind the wheel of our driveReport car quickly conveyed the feeling that it is not in any way seriously outdated or outclassed by the latest Corvettes. Its owner since May 1972 has been Dr. William Lado, a dentist whose practice is located in Oneonta, New York. When Lado purchased the car it was still under the original five year-50,000 mile warranty. It still has been driven less than 35,000 miles. Originally Lado's Corvette was equipped with the side exhaust system first available on the 1965 models. The appearance of the side pipes was in keeping with the performance capability of the car, but to Lado's way of

thinking they were "just too loud." On trips of any length he describes their sound as a "reverberating horror." "No person in his right mind," says Lado, "would put up with the noise." After two years of trying to live with them, Lado had them replaced late in 1974 with the standard exhaust system.

On the road the performance of this Corvette borders on the supernatural. With its vacuum operated triple carburetor system there is not the sudden violent unleashing of power that characterized tri-powered units that were mechanically connected. Instead the turbine-like acceleration and smoothness of the old fuel injected Corvettes is very closely duplicated by this engine when it is given its head. The only difference is that it is far more powerful than any stock Corvette with fuel injection. Chevrolet advertised this engine as developing 435 horsepower at 5800 rpm. However, its redline is pegged at 6500 rpm and probably a more accurate assessment of its power output would be in the 475-485 horsepower range.

Driving such a car (with its Marlboro Maroon finish it's only slightly less conspicuous than a formula one racing car in this rural area of upstate New York) means that if the driver is so inclined he can spend all day engaging in the great American pastime of street racing. Bill Lado says he is "challenged

all the time" and to date has never been beaten in any impromptu traffic-light showdown. However, he also admits that he has never encountered a Cobra.

Aside from the astounding performance ability of this car, its most desirable feature is its appearance. Unlike most automobiles that in their final facelifting seem to lose most of their initial attractiveness, the 1967 Corvette was the cleanest, meanest and leanest-appearing of the first generation Sting Rays. Although those powered by the Mark IV 427-cid engines had false hood scoops, they are, overall, free of any artificiality and the numerous superfluous trim items found in earlier models. Moreover, the impression that this is a thoroughbred sports car is not merely visual. In such small items as its recessed sun visors and console-mounted emergency brake, the '67 Sting Ray reflects the ultimate maturation of its design. In contrast to the '67's coordinated and well-assembled design, the 1963 Sting Ray appears almost crude and unfinished.

Total production of 1967 Sting Rays amounted to 22,940 (8504 of which were coupes), down from the 1966 mark of 27,720.

Ken Purdy's classic book was entitled *Kings of the Road*. While not born of aristocratic parents, the Corvette Sting Rays also seem worthy of a similar title. □

Spotter's Guide
1963-'67 Corvette

by Jeff Godshall

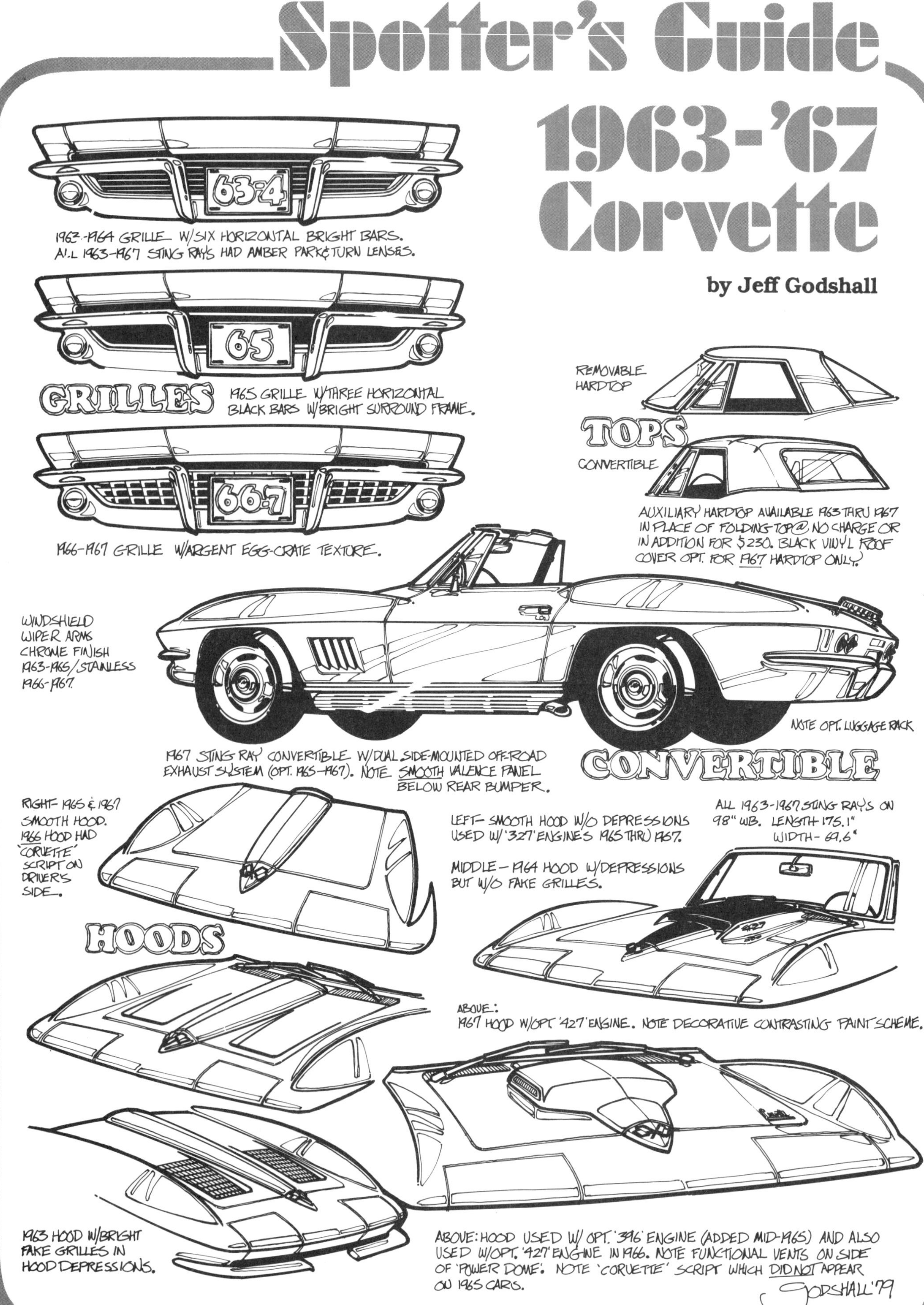

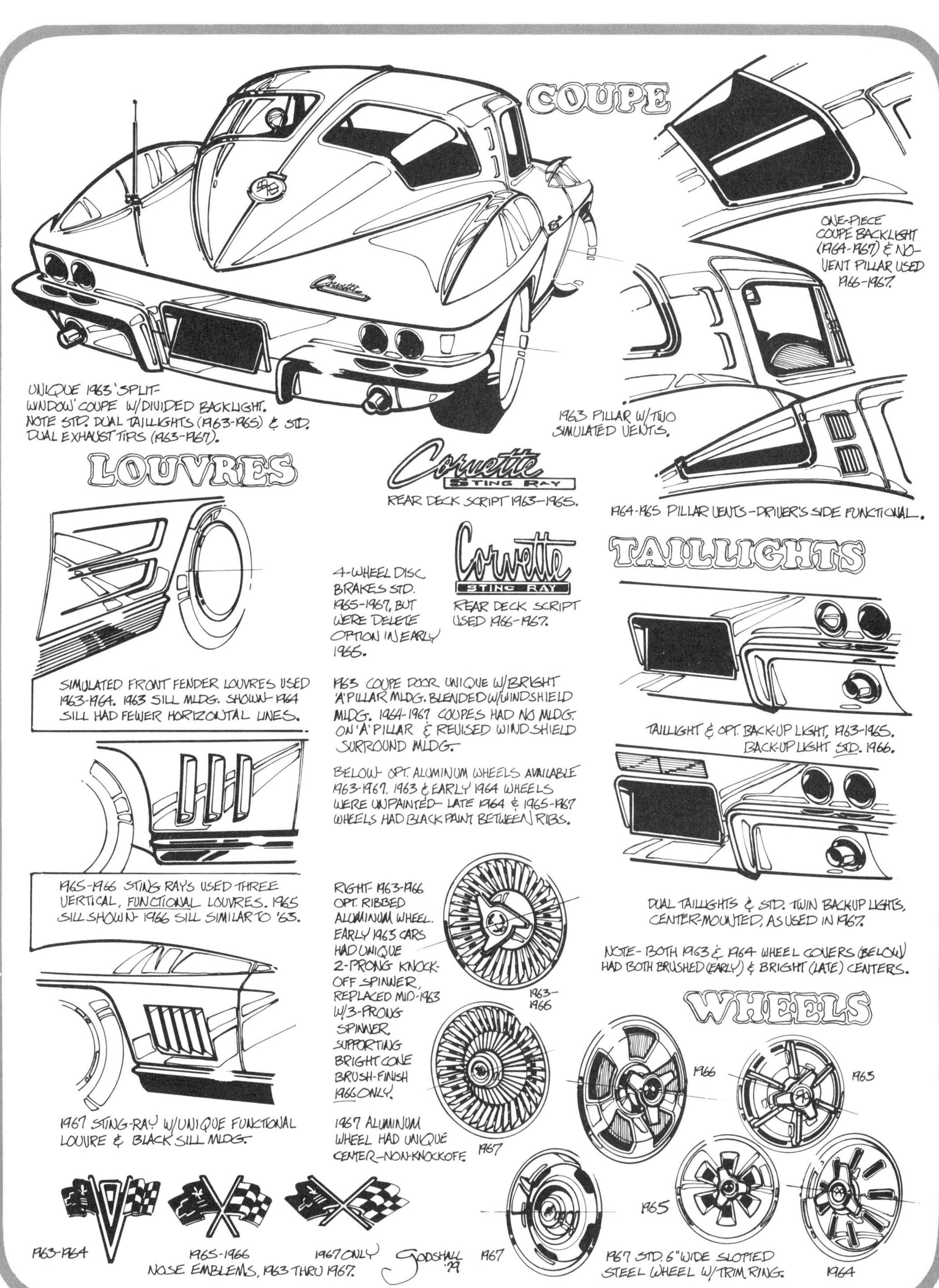

COUPE

ONE-PIECE COUPE BACKLIGHT (1964-1967) & NO-VENT PILLAR USED 1966-1967.

1963 PILLAR W/TWO SIMULATED VENTS.

UNIQUE 1963 'SPLIT-WINDOW' COUPE W/DIVIDED BACKLIGHT. NOTE STD. DUAL TAILLIGHTS (1963-1965) & STD. DUAL EXHAUST TIPS (1963-1967).

1964-1965 PILLAR VENTS-DRIVER'S SIDE FUNCTIONAL.

LOUVRES

Corvette STING RAY
REAR DECK SCRIPT 1963-1965.

TAILLIGHTS

SIMULATED FRONT FENDER LOUVRES USED 1963-1964. 1963 SILL MLDG. SHOWN-1964 SILL HAD FEWER HORIZONTAL LINES.

4-WHEEL DISC BRAKES STD. 1965-1967, BUT WERE DELETE OPTION IN EARLY 1965.

Corvette STING RAY
REAR DECK SCRIPT USED 1966-1967.

1963 COUPE DOOR UNIQUE W/BRIGHT 'A' PILLAR MLDG. BLENDED W/WINDSHIELD MLDG. 1964-1967 COUPES HAD NO MLDG. ON 'A' PILLAR & REVISED WINDSHIELD SURROUND MLDG.

TAILLIGHT & OPT. BACK-UP LIGHT, 1963-1965. BACK-UP LIGHT STD. 1966.

BELOW OPT. ALUMINUM WHEELS AVAILABLE 1963-1967. 1963 & EARLY 1964 WHEELS WERE UNPAINTED- LATE 1964 & 1965-1967 WHEELS HAD BLACK PAINT BETWEEN RIBS.

1965-1966 STING RAY'S USED THREE VERTICAL, FUNCTIONAL LOUVRES. 1965 SILL SHOWN-1966 SILL SIMILAR TO '63.

RIGHT 1963-1966 OPT. RIBBED ALUMINUM WHEEL. EARLY 1963 CARS HAD UNIQUE 2-PRONG KNOCK-OFF SPINNER, REPLACED MID-1963 W/3-PRONG SPINNER SUPPORTING BRIGHT CONE BRUSH-FINISH 1966 ONLY.

1963-1966

DUAL TAILLIGHTS & STD. TWIN BACKUP LIGHTS, CENTER-MOUNTED, AS USED IN 1967.

NOTE- BOTH 1963 & 1964 WHEEL COVERS (BELOW) HAD BOTH BRUSHED (EARLY) & BRIGHT (LATE) CENTERS.

WHEELS

1966

1963

1967 STING-RAY W/UNIQUE FUNCTIONAL LOUVRE & BLACK SILL MLDG.

1967 ALUMINUM WHEEL HAD UNIQUE CENTER-NON-KNOCKOFF

1967

1965

1963-1964

1965-1966

1967 ONLY

Godshall '79

1967

NOSE EMBLEMS, 1963 THRU 1967.

1967 STD. 6" WIDE SLOTTED STEEL WHEEL W/TRIM RING.

1964

1968 CORVETTE

A SECOND RABBIT FROM THE SAME HAT

by J. William Lamm
photos by the author

THE Corvette Sting Ray — a gorgeous, graceful, innovative design — had been out for less than a year in 1964. It was sleek, unique, and selling like crazy. It was also on death row.

GM had given it a sales lifespan of about four years. So when 1964 rolled around, and the Sting Ray was still an infant, GM's design chief William L. Mitchell was already looking toward the '67 debut of a brand new body. Back then, beauty didn't count much towards longevity.

Mitchell had to have a theme chosen and rolling by 1965, and that wouldn't have been easy under *any* conditions. But being the man responsible for the Corvette that was *currently* doing so well, he put some extra heat on the situation. To make the new car a winner, Bill Mitchell would have to top the one designer he wasn't sure *could*

Driving Impressions

In the days of the big-block, party talk was usually about how fast your car could do the quarter-mile. In the fuel-injected world of today, though, things like handling, braking, and structural integrity have worked their way into the conversation. Whether we've lost or gained for it all is a personal decision.

I do know, by coming straight from the wheel of a 1988 Corvette Z52 to the '68 big-block, that the old 'Vette comes from a world long gone. Where the current model is tight, solid, and reassuringly quick, the '68 is loose, willowy, and blindingly fast — at least on straight pavement.

At anything above a mild clip, each turn entered in the '68 is a workout for the elbows, eyes, and nerves. Its nose-full of engine plows merrily on until you literally snap it away from dead-center. Then, once committed, you're left to herd the car back and forth, back and forth, until finally the road appears more or less between the fenders again. Then nail the gas and BAM! You're making up whatever time you lost, and darn fast.

Driving twisty roads in the big-block Corvette is like cutting canteloupe with a sledgehammer — an inelegant solution, but one that certainly gets the job done. The same's true for its performance in traffic. Heat from the engine bay percolates the

driver's tootsies, the stiff controls make your right arm and left leg ache, and keeping a constant eye on the temperature gauge leaves your nerves on edge. You do, however, get where you're going before anyone else.

Of course, the big-block was never meant to be driven in the real world. Even the power-hungry enthusiast press came right out and said it: Get a small-block if you want a car. Get a big-block if you want America's #1 toy. In all fairness, though, a number of two-liter foreign jobs will boil toes and glycol as quickly as the seven-liter 'Vette. And its bendable body and hunt-and-peck suspension are indicative of all '68-era convertibles, not just this one. (Unfortunately, its brakes are, well...as the saying goes, you don't buy a Corvette to *slow down*.)

Some parts of the car are simply excellent. The non-adjustable seats are comfortable and give lots of support. The telescoping wheel is handy. And the four-speed manual transmission is particularly fine — with short, quick throws, it rewards a firm hand with the sound and feel of gears meshing into place.

And then, of course, there's the acceleration. Most people accept that the big-block Corvette was merely Chevy's sacrifice to the quarter-mile gods. Thirteen-second

drag times made up for a lot of sins in '68. The famous 427 engine is an amazing machine: It jacks the car ten degrees to the right, puts a goofy grin on the most stoic faces, and consumes pavement and fuel in magnificent great gulps. In many ways, the 427 makes this car *too* fast: too fast for its brakes, too fast for its tires, and too fast for most of its drivers. I have yet to hear one complain, however.

When all is said and done, this is one car that really *wants* to cooperate. If the job is passing turnip trucks, the Corvette says "no problem." Two inches of toe travel and there's one less truck in your way. While you're often fighting *with* this car, rarely do you fight *against* it. It's as though driver and car are teamed up against a common foe — like one of those evil 90-degree turns.

Corvettes have always been cars that some people will love and others will hate. The 427 is no exception. An equal number of those praising its straight-line performance will damn its jittery cornering. For every person who respects the innovation of its design, there's another whose eyes see just another model of the "14-year Corvette."

Whatever your own feelings on the big-block may be, there's no denying that the folks who love it have ample grounds.

1968 CORVETTE

Above: Swing-up headlamps are vacuum-operated; were tested by Chevrolet to be able to break through ⅜-inch sheet of ice covering. *Below:* 427 engines have their own special hood design to help clear the big powerhouse. *Above right:* driveReport car uses standard '68 wheel discs.

be topped: Bill Mitchell. It was an unspoken fact, known to all, that the '67 would have to be one heck of a design to hold its own against the '63.

To get right to the meat of the story, Mitchell's staff found that winning shape in two places. Much of the "feel" of the car, in the view of Mitchell's right-hand-man, Larry Shinoda, came from the XP-819, a GM experimental powered by a *rear-mounted,* all-aluminum Chevy V-8. (Despite the fact that the XP-819 drove pretty nicely, GM's engineers were understandably nervous about continuing with a car that had 80 percent of its weight on the rear tires.)

Using the 819 as a starting — and as a falling back — point, the development of the new Corvette body began in earnest with something Mitchell had asked of his designers. Larry Shinoda remembers that request: "Give me a Formula One car that you could stick two people in, [with] big bulged-out fenders." And that was exactly what they did. Shinoda and his own assistant, John Schinella, did some cartoon-like renderings of cars with low, sleek bodies and big, almost pontoon fenders. "We showed him those," Shinoda laughs, "and he just *had* to have them. The more we put in the fenders, the more he liked it."

When the time came to give up the cartoons and start some serious designing, the fenders became more integrated with the body, but they still remained the dominant feature of the design. The graceful, vestigial sweeps above the wheel wells of the original Sting Ray became the now-familiar scooped haunches seen on every 'Vette from 1968 to 1982.

Mitchell took one look at these more serious sketches and knew that he'd found his shape. The theme was exciting, racy, and above all *fresh*; it owed nothing to the competition, and just enough to the previous Sting Ray to let everyone know that this car was,indeed, a true Corvette.

To add impact to the aggressive fenders, the hoodline between them was

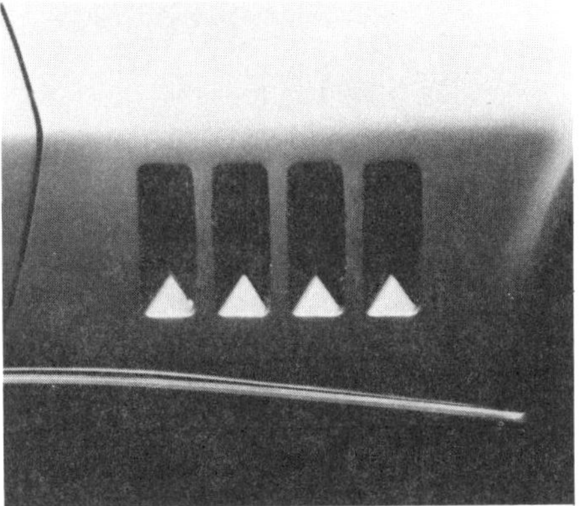

*Above: Bulgy, prominent fender lines and pinched-in passenger compartment are part of William L. Mitchell's styling trademarks during his reign as GM styling chief. **Below left:** Vertical fender scoops first appeared on 1965 Corvettes. **Right:** Outside handles blend smoothly into door kickup. **Bottom:** No mistaking which powerplant lurks under the hood!*

made as low as possible (lower than possible, it turned out), and the car's midsection tapered in toward the rear of the doors. A raked windshield led to a removable roof, in turn leading to a sloping rear end, and at the back everything met in a rounded tail and fashionable spoiler.

Finished and molded in fiberglass, it was the Mako Shark II, one of GM's most significant — and complex, and expensive, and publicized — showcars of all time. Two of them would eventually be built: a display version without running gear, and a "driver" made from a '65 Corvette chassis and the soon-to-be-available 427-inch engine. The Mako Shark II went public in 1965 and was an immediate smash.

Even without its radical lines, the Mako Shark II couldn't have helped drawing a crowd. It had so many tricks and trap doors it made some of the gadget-laden showcars of the Motorama's glory years seem downright Spartan in comparison. There were power-operated doors covering the turning and brake lights and hiding the wipers; a one-piece removable roof and a fully-opening clamshell hood; elaborately finned sidepipes on the non-running car, designed with great effort by Schinella, and an early application of digital instruments on the runner. And, of course, the Mako II had a constant escort of pretty models in tight sweaters, sporting the kind of chests that only today men are realizing weren't quite the way nature had intended. (The list of

specifications

© copyright 1989, Special Interest Autos

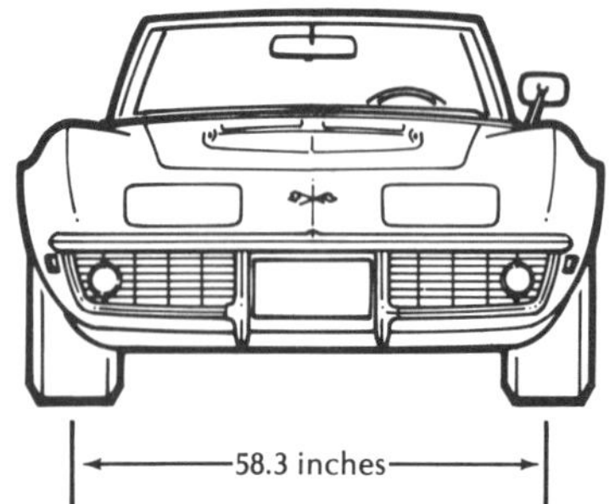

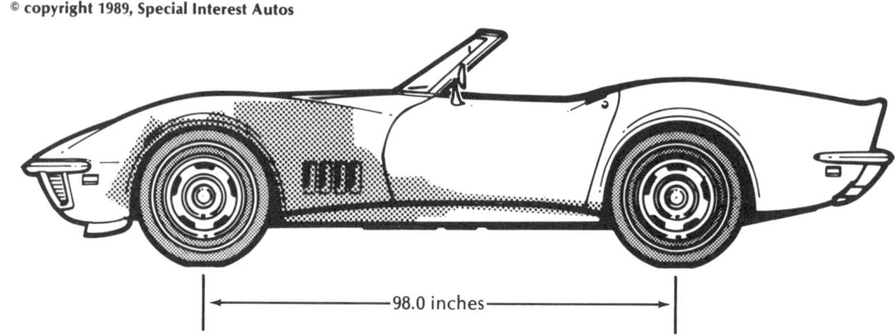

1968 Corvette

Price when new	$6,142
Estimated value today	$12,750/$19,500

ENGINE
Type	Ohv V-8, cast-iron alloy block and cylinder heads
Bore x stroke	4.25 inches x 3.76 inches
Displacement	427 cubic inches (6,997 cc)
HP @ rpm	435 @ 5,800
Torque @ rpm	460 @ 4,000
Compression ratio	11.0:1
Induction system	Three 2-bbl Holley
Electrical system	Delco-Remy 12V, neg. ground

TRANSMISSION
Type	4-speed manual, synchro in all forward gears
Ratios: 1st	2.20:1
2nd	1.64:1
3rd	1.27:1
4th	1.00:1
5th (or 4th OD)	N/a
Reverse	2.26:1

CLUTCH
Type	Single-plate dry disc-type, 11.0-inch O.D., diaphragm pressure plate

DIFFERENTIAL
Type	Sprung differential, hypoid gears, limited slip design
Ratio	3.55:1

STEERING
Type	Saginaw-built recirculating ball
Turns lock-to-lock	2.9
Turning radius	39.9 feet

BRAKES
Type	Vented discs front and rear, optional power assist
Diameter, f/r	11.8 inches/11.8 inches
Total swept area	259 square inches/ton, 461.2 inches total

CHASSIS & BODY
Construction	Fiberglass over steel skeleton
Frame	Full-length ladder-type frame, 5 crossmembers
Body style	Convertible, 2-door/2-pass., canvas or fiberglass roof std, both available at extra cost

SUSPENSION
Front	Unequal-length A-arms w/ tube shocks, coil springs, anti-roll bar (independent type suspension)
Rear	Trailing arms, toe links, transverse chromium-carbon steel leaf spring, tube shocks, anti-roll bar (independent type suspension)
Tires	F70-15 (Firestone Super Sport Wide Ovals OEM)
Wheels	15x7JK (steel)

WEIGHTS AND MEASURES
Wheelbase	98.0 inches
Overall length	182.1 inches
Overall height	48.6 inches
Overall width	69.2 inches
Front track	58.3 inches
Rear track	59.0 inches
Curb weight	3,285 pounds (with lightest option list, not including L88 aluminum 427). Test weight closer to 3,600 pounds (w/fluids)

PERFORMANCE
0-30	3.0 seconds
0-50	5.3 seconds
0-60	6.5 seconds
¼ mile	13.41 seconds @ 109.5 mph
Top speed	142 mph with listed powertrain

Specs courtesy AMA listings released 10/15/67.

This page: Fuel filler cap is symmetrically if inconveniently placed on rear deck. Facing page, top left: Sign of the times: Engine plate has anti-pollution tuneup instructions. Top right: Full complement of analog gauges occupy center console. Above center: Dual taillamp theme was carryover from Sting Ray. Center: Top folds up and hides under fiberglass swing-up boot. Bottom: 1968 design caused nearly as much of a sensation when new as the '63 Sting Ray and set the basic Corvette shape through 1977.

1968 CORVETTE

gadgets goes on and on, but we'll stop at the models like everyone else.)

Not a gadget per se, more a "gimmick," was the Mako II's paint job, a mini-masterstroke in its own right. Cued from a real shark, it fogged from dark blue upper surfaces to white below. More than a mimic of nature, this scheme kept the chiseled lower half of the car from being lost in shadows when photographed. Mitchell insisted on the finish, knowing that better photos would mean more coverage; the sort of thinking that made him the boss.

In the true vein of showcars, only a few of the Mako II's tricks — like the vacuum-powered wiper panel — made it to the real Corvette in 1968. And of those that didn't, most weren't worth mourning. Some, however, like the clamshell hood and "soft" body-color front and rear caps, would have been welcome had the technology and funding been available at the time.

With the Mako behind him, Mitchell could take a quick breather. But the fight for the new Corvette was far from over; the entire tail, starting at the leading edge of the rear fenders, would eventually be redesigned. Alan Young is given much of the credit for that excellent job. The new rear-end shape was as clean and elegant as the front was aggressive, with flying buttresses similar to those on Ferrari and Porsche racing cars replacing the never-quite-there sloping cockpit of the Mako, and the tailpiece cleaned up and shortened.

But try as the designers might, the car simply refused to be ready by the 1967 target date. John Schinella (today head of GM's Advanced Concepts Center in California) explains the delay simply as one of refinement, to, in his words, "make sure the car was right."

But Zora Arkus-Duntov (then the program's chief engineer and now known simply as the "Father of the Corvette") puts it a little more strongly. "[In 1967], the car was not fit to drive on the street."

Duntov recalls particularly that the top few inches of the front fenders caused a visibility problem that he found unacceptable, and he demanded — and got — them changed. Schinella recalls the complaint but not the fix. Regardless, Duntov continues, "Styling was instructed to tone down the car. We kept the structure intact, but changed the outer surfaces a little.

"Larry Shinoda was instrumental in [this]. And the '68 car, as you know, was very agreeable. So, I was agreeable and Pete Estes [then head of Chevrolet] was agreeable."

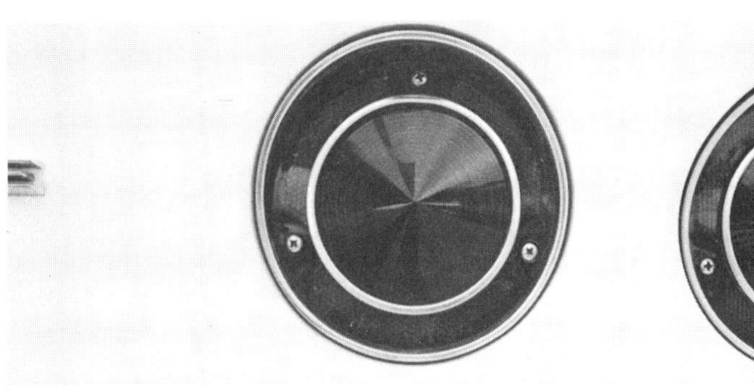

Above: Abundantly powerful 427-cubic-inch engine could propel driveReport car just a shade past 140 mph. Below: It looks almost as aggressive in the back as it does out front.

1968 CORVETTE

Duntov and Mitchell had many times before been locked in friendly, but intense, combat over the Corvette, arguing the classic conflict of form versus function or, more precisely, styling versus engineering. This round was to go to Duntov, and model-year 1967 would indeed be spent refining the car for an introduction date pushed back to '68.

An all-new interior, a blend of Mako Shark II and standard GM, came with the new body. It was clean and simple, sporting Astro (flow-through) Ventilation, a mandatory console, and fiber-optic cables to show the condition of running and brake lights to the driver inside the cockpit. Again, Duntov had worries: The ancillary gauges were all grouped in a center console, where they couldn't be seen without taking the driver's eyes off the road. That round, however, would go to the stylists.

Under the new-for-'68 skin was the same excellent twin-rail frame and all-independent suspension that Corvettes had ridden on since 1963. Also, the same engines available for '67 (327s with 300 or 350 horses, and 427s with 390, 400, or 435) could be had in 1968.

Though collectors prize the big-block

And As If Acne, Girls, And Grades Weren't Enough....

As I entered puberty, my car-nut father entered his Musclecar Period. In the regular parade of tatty project cars, Hudsons and their like gave way to a bought-and-sold stream of sixties and seventies vintage musclecars. Offhand, I remember a GTO, a couple of Camaros, a Mustang, a 455 Trans Am, and a Firebird 400 (which later became a star...see *SIA #95*).

Today, I often reflect on the lunacy of a man with teenage sons who knowingly purchased such cars.

The zenith — and, in retrospect, end — of the Musclecar Period was a Corvette. A '68 Roadster, with a 427, a four-speed close-ratio box, and...well, you see what I'm getting at.

It's an old story. A child gets his first driver's license and his father owns a Corvette. His mother notices strange saliva stains on the front of his shirts, and his teachers start to worry about his distracted behavior. Is it girls?...drugs?...is he hanging out with the wrong crowd?

It was, in fact, the automotive equivalent of all three. A car like a Corvette — particularly like *that* Corvette — speaks to the 16-year-old in everyone. If you happen to be a walking, talking, *real-life* 16-year-old, it grabs your lapels, shakes you back and forth, and screams "HEY, YOU IDIOT, DON'T JUST STAND THERE; LET'S *GO!*"

Now if the three of us kids had been instructed to treat the Corvette as if it were a typhoid carrier, there's no doubt that

sooner or later I'd have had to sneak it out. It's another old story: The parents go on vacation, the kid sneaks the 'Vette out, crashes, and has to move to Peru under an assumed name.

Conversely, had we been given free reign with the car, *its* fate would have been the same. The trip to the Andes might have been delayed a month or two, but that would have happened, too.

So we got the car in small doses, always with the old man planted firmly in the passenger's seat. Every month, I'd get a month's worth of Corvette out of my system.

But my first time in the car was the best. I wanted to learn to drive with three pedals, and my father suggested the Corvette, saying it would be the hardest one to stall. (Looking back, he must have been in some kind of trance; maybe he'd looked into the chrome fan blades while the engine was running.)

But whatever the reason, there I was. First gear, toward me and up. Yeah, that's first. Okay.

I revved the engine and let out the clutch. Pretty slowly, too...the car squealed, shuddered, and bellowed, the engine raced and the tach rolled to 5,500. Somewhere in my confusion, the tires hooked up and the car launched forward.

Second gear was more of the same. Whether the tight feeling in my neck was

due to acceleration or wishful thinking from my father, I can't say.

The clutch went again, but I couldn't find third. I coasted to the next stop sign. I paused while my stomach caught up to the car, thoughtfully carrying my heart-rate and eyeballs under one arm.

"Gee, Dad...." I mustered my best no-smirk deadpan. "That's pretty fast."

"Yep. You ought to see it in first and second."

The Corvette's been gone for years now, and my affection for 'Vettes in general has waxed and waned and waxed again in the meantime. It was hot back when I was 16, but cooled off a bit in the period between my discoveries of corners and throttle steer. It went colder still when I met a girl with a Silver Anniversary (1978) coupe — a fine car in its own right, but terribly slow and soft compared to the '68; more a touring car than a ride for hormone-charged teenagers. (Which, I suppose, is actually a compliment.)

And now my enthusiasm's become red-hot again, with the arrival of the current convertible and a new-found eye for the '63-67 Sting Rays.

And even if the '68 isn't my first pick in a Corvette today, it's a moot point. But if youthful enthusiasm gives way to nostalgic longing at about the same time being an impoverished writer gives way to being a guy with a *real* job, well then there may well be a '68 roadster in my future yet.

cars today, their smaller brothers offered much more practicality for road use. True, the monster 435-horse 427 (with three two-barrel carbs and, early on, aluminum heads) gave blinding acceleration, but only at a considerable cost to economy, tractability, and handling. Road testers of the day generally recommended the seven-liter engines only for those who planned to drag race their cars. For everyone else, they felt the 350- and even 300-horse small-block made more sense, providing plenty of power with good manners to boot.

Paralleling the large choice of engines, the buyer could select a manual or automatic transmission, wide or close gear spacing, and a number of rear axle ratios. Completing the list of major options were air conditioning; power windows, brakes, and steering; an AM/FM stereo; and the convertible buyer's choice of hard top, soft top, or both.

Even though the car was well received by the public, for the most part the '68 took its lumps at the hands of magazine editors. Complaints cited a noisy engine, smaller-than-'67 cockpit, larger overall size, poor ventilation, and generally spotty construction quality, and in many ways these were all valid gripes.

But worst of all, the styling of the car was met with decidedly mixed emotions. *Road & Track* (1/68) had one of the less favorable opinions, stating, "One almost expects strobe lights to come up when those monstrous flaps out front start lifting at the pull of the headlight switch. Chevrolet stylists have sensed...the fads of the day."

The '68 certainly deserved some of the abuse it took. It was plagued with squeaks and rattles, poorly calibrated power accessories, and chronic over-

*Left: Mako Shark II would be a fresh design even in 1989. **Above:** Mako's styling touches are obvious in production car. **Below left:** The shark was a favorite design theme of Mitchell. He even had one stuffed and mounted in his office! **Below right:** Rearend design of Mako is thoroughly modern despite being over two decades old.*

1968 CORVETTE

heating, all of which were addressed in the next model year. For owners of the '68, of course, that was no consolation, and Chevrolet would be embarrassed about the development problems for some time.

But it's quite easy to make the case that the Corvette was (and is) also a "whipping boy" for many magazines dissatisfied with the American industry in general. The chassis, hailed as state-of-the-art in '63, was called outmoded in '68, although very little street-bound machinery had come along to challenge it in those five years. And in any article berating the '68, you'll find that only after lambasting the car's flaws for the first three pages do the last few paragraphs admit that the Corvette was, in fact, one of the best handling, fastest, and toughest cars on the market. (It was rarely mentioned that it was also three or four times cheaper than any other cars in the same performance league.)

The American press has often been unkind to the Corvette, and at times it's been deservedly so. But to forget what one is dealing with — an *affordable, reliable* performance car — is shoddy journalism. To forget that the Corvette's performance was often superior to the competition *regardless* of price and durability is downright snobbery. □

Acknowledgements and Bibliography
Corvette: America's Only True Sports Car; The Genuine Corvette Black Book 1953-1984; "Mako Shark II: The Perfect Dream Car," Corvette! The Sensuous American 1983 - #2; *Ray Miller,* The Real Corvette; Motor Trend World Automotive Yearbook 1968; Corvette: An American Classic; "350-hp Corvette," Road & Track, 1/68; "435-hp Corvette," Road & Track, 3/69; "Four Luxury GTs," Road & Track, 6/69; Arthur A.C. Steffen, Corvette 1968-1982: A Source Book; "Corvette Duet: Chamber Music and Hard Rock," Car Life, June 1968.
Thanks to Michael Antonick, Brad Arnold, Ron Bailey, Kurtis R. Bosacki, CPC Engineering, Jack Case, Corvette California, Corvette World, Diablo Valley Corvettes, Zora Duntov, Floyd Joliet, Lodi Corvette Club, Reno Lucchesi, Hal Malone, Michael Bruce Associates, Ed Ryan, John Schinella, Larry Shinoda, and Specialty Sales of Pleasanton, California.

1969 ZL-1 CORVETTE

CHEVY'S ULTIMATE POWER TRIP

by Dave Emanuel
photos by the author

IT HAD been building for quite some time, since 1955 actually. And with each passing year, the melody grew progressively louder. By the early sixties, the previously random sounds had been wrought into harmony, and with the groundwork established, Chevrolet Motor Division began orchestrating a symphony of unmitigated horsepower.

Surreptitiously, of course. By corporate edict, the division could not openly engage in auto racing, so the symphony was played in a private auditorium, and those who were privileged enough to be invited to listen, arrived through the back, rather than the front door. Year after year, the members of the orchestra honed their skills and the symphony climaxed in ever-greater crescendo. Then in 1969 came the *crescendo magnifico*, a ground-shaking explosion known as the ZL-1. An all-aluminum 427 developed expressly for Can-Am road racing, the engine was never officially given a horsepower rating. But estimates placed the figure at over 600. And on rare occasion, a Corvette fitted with the burly ZL-1 powerplant was unleashed to roam the streets as an allegedly legitimate passenger car.

The clandestine engineering effort that culminated in the ZL-1 began with the introduction of the first production Mark IV which debuted in the 1965 Corvette. Prototypes, in various configurations, had previously been seen as early as 1963 on the NASCAR circuit, and the canted-valve arrangement had given rise to the term "Porcupine head." But few people actually saw these powerplants and the shroud of secrecy that surrounded them led to a rather apropos moniker — "Mystery Engine."

It was therefore with great eagerness that the debut of the production version was anticipated. Midway through the 1965 model year, the mystery was no more. Chevrolet pulled the wraps away with the announcement of a 396-cubic-inch (4.09-inch bore, 3.76-inch stroke) "Turbo-Jet" engine as optional equipment for the full-sized Chevrolet and Corvette. (It was also available in a limited number of Chevelle Super Sports (see *SIA* #71). In its most robust state of tune, with 11:1 compression ratio, large-port cylinder heads, high-lift mechanical cam and a Holley four-barrel atop a high rise aluminum intake manifold, the engine produced 425 horsepower at 6,400 rpm and 415 lbs./ft. torque at 4,000 rpm. It was the first large-block powerplant ever installed in America's only sports car and also had the distinction of being the most brutally powerful engine Chevrolet had ever placed in the engine compartment of a production Corvette. In its test of the car, *Road & Track* stated, "It's an interesting technical exercise, building a nice big engine like the 396 and putting it in a good chassis like the Corvette, but it honestly isn't a very satisfactory car for driving in everyday traffic. It's too much of a brute for that. And with all that power, any manner in which it is driven on anything except dead dry paving, the car is going to be a very large handful. It is not a car for the inexpert or the inattentive — two blinks of the eye and a careless poke of the toe and you could be in serious trouble."

One can only conjure the scene when the author of *Road & Track*'s test returned to the office, with hands shaking, knees trembling and undergarments in

This page, right: *The monster motor. Better than one horsepower for each of its 427 cubic inches and a relentless thirst for super high-octane gas with its 12.5:1 compression ratio.* ***Below:*** *Car was subjected to a frame-up restoration. Most difficult task was finding the original engine block, which had been removed from the car years before and had literally disappeared.* ***Facing page, top:*** *Body was in good condition but received concours paint treatment nevertheless.*

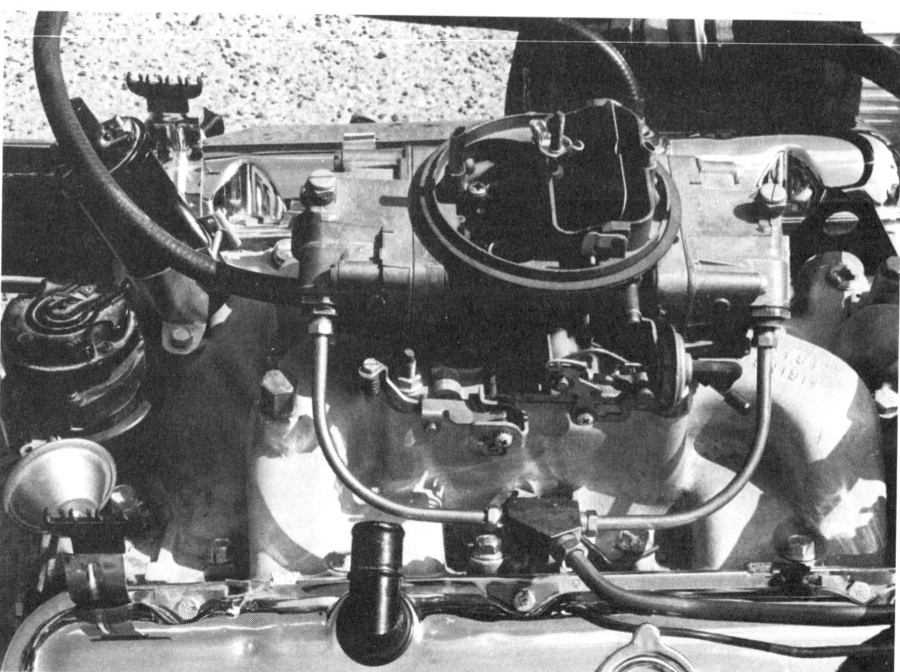

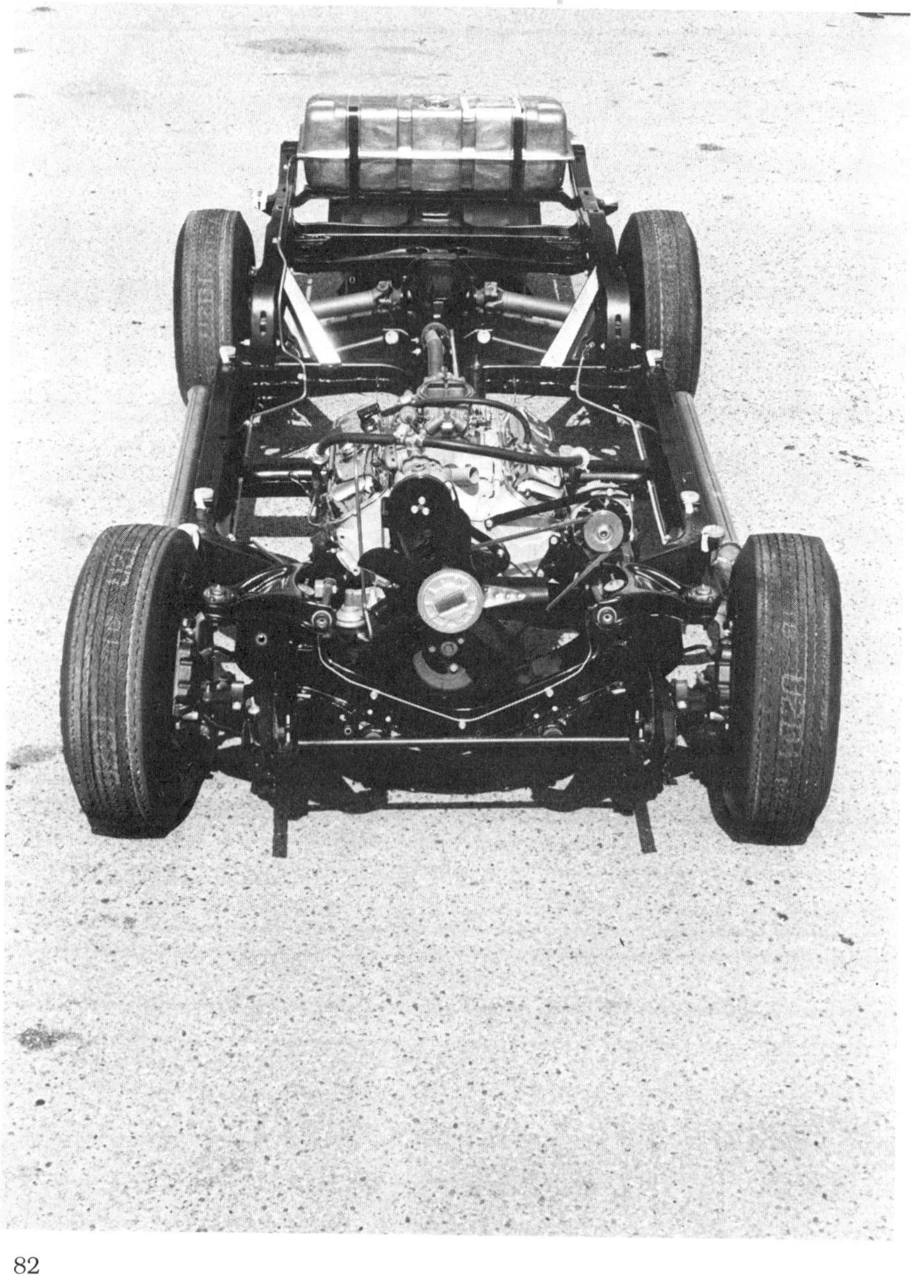

need of replacement, but the 396 paled in comparison to the even more brutish 427 that was released the following year. Once again, the most powerful engine in the Corvette stable was rated at 425 horsepower, but the displacement had been bumped 31 cubic inches by virtue of a 5/32-inch overbore. (Not too surprisingly, *Road & Track* avoided testing the 427 for several years.) With all internal components being virtually identical between the 396 and 427 (the obvious exception being the pistons), it was quite apparent that the horsepower ratings were about as accurate as a summer weather forecast in Texas. But there was a reasonable explanation for

Corvette '69

ZL1-688

Daytona yellow. Special Turbo-jet 427 CID, aluminum cylinder block, special 4 speed transmission, full transistor ignition, PT axle, 4.11 ratio, special brake system, side mount exhaust, tilt steering wheel, audio alarm system, special purpose suspension. A one of a kind item. List $10,773.65. See or call Charlie Conover.

Hechler

CHEVROLET

Nine Mile Rd. at Eastgate
222-3533 Dealer 122

COUGAR — '68, factory air and warranty, 2-door hardtop, low down payment, 233-8311, Dealer 3701.

COUGAR — '67, 298, automatic, power steering and brakes, gold, vin... $1595. 746-516 Dealer ...

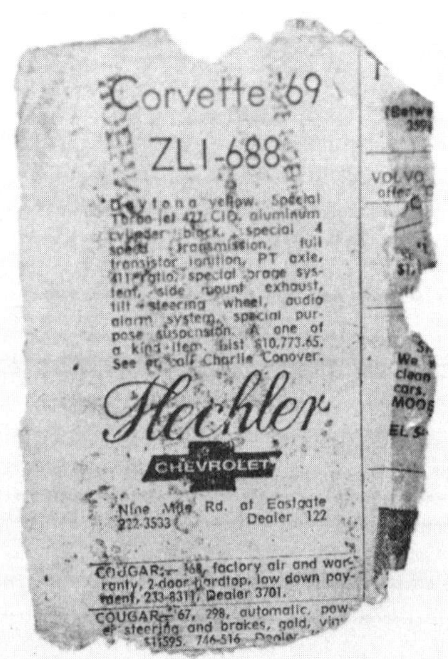

Richmond, Virginia, Chevy dealer first offered our feature car in 1969. Price tag of over ten grand, cheap for a new sports car today, was stratospheric back in that pre-inflation era.

the creative accounting being done by the engineering department. At the time, General Motors corporate policy simply made any number in excess of 425 verboten, so the 427 was rated at 5,600 rpm, well below the 6,400-6,500 rpm power peak where it reportedly produced over 450 horsepower.

The 427 quickly earned its stripes on the race course, but the Ford-equipped Cobra remained a force to be reckoned with—a thorn in the side of Corvette racers. Chevrolet engineering began an assault on the Cobra's supremacy in earnest in 1967. It culminated in RPO (regular production option) L-88, which consisted of a cast-iron 427 equipped with aluminum cylinder heads, 12.5:1 compression ratio, high-rise aluminum intake manifold and Holley 850 CFM four-barrel carburetor.

The L-88 Corvettes were no more than race cars offered to the public in sufficient numbers to enable them to be classified as production cars for competition purposes. And compete they did. According to Karl Ludvigsen in his book *Corvette: America's Star Spangled Sports Car*, at the 1967 running of the 24 Hours of Le Mans, an L-88 driven by Bob Bondurant and Dick Guldstrand was clocked at 171.5 miles per hour on the long Mulsanne Straight. (In an interview in *Vette Vues* magazine, Cliff Gottlob, who ran 186 miles per hour in an L-88 at Daytona, stated, "The books say 171, but 191 is more like it.") The car led the Ferraris and other marques competing in the GT class by such a wide margin that during the first 11 hours the race was a nine-course dinner of humble pie for the Corvette's competitors. Then, not quite halfway through the event, the engine expired, putting the car out of the race. But the

1969 ZL-1 Corvette Specifications

Price	$4,927.50
As equipped	$10,773
Optional equipment	Special Turbo-Jet 427 engine, transistor ignition, Positraction rear axle with 4.11:1 ratio, close ratio 4-speed transmission, F70x15 white lettered tires, tinted glass, special-purpose suspension, special brake system, side-mounted exhaust, tilt-telescoping steering wheel, front fender louver trim, audio alarm system, aluminum cylinder block
Engine type	V-8 ohv
Bore and stroke	4.25 x 3.76
Displacement	427 cubic inches
Horsepower	430 @ 5,200 rpm
Torque	450 @ 4,400 rpm
Compression ratio	12.5:
Induction	Holley 850 CFM 4-bbl on aluminum manifold
Exhaust system	Dual, 2.5-inch diameter
Electrical system	12-volt battery/coil
Transmission type	4-speed manual
Ratios: 1st	2.20:1
2nd	1.64:1
3rd	1.27:1
4th	1:1
Differential type	Hypoid semi-floating, limited slip
Ratio	4.11:1
Steering type	Semi-reversible, recirculating ball, power assisted
Ratio	17.6:1
Turns lock to lock	2.9
Turning circle	39.0 feet
Brakes, type	Hydraulic with vacuum power assist, 11.75-inch diameter ventilated discs front and rear
Total swept area	461 square inches
Chassis and body construction	Welded steel ladder frame
Body	Fiberglass 2-door coupe
Front suspension	Independent SLA, coil springs, double-acting tubular shocks, anti-sway bar
Rear suspension	Independent with lateral leaf spring, lateral struts double-acting tubular shocks, stabilizer bar
Wheels	15-inch x 8-inch slotted steel disc
Tires	F70x15-inch 2-ply white lettered
Dimensions, Wheelbase	98.0 inches
Overall length	182.5 inches
Overall height	47.9 inches
Overall width	69.0 inches
Front track	58.7 inches
Rear track	59.4 inches
Curb weight	3,200 pounds
Performance: maximum speed	130+ (with 4.11:1 axle ratio)
Acceleration: standing start ¼-mile	12.1 seconds and 116 mph
Fuel economy	Don't ask

Americans *had* made their presence felt.

Although considered a regular production option, the L-88 was produced in severely limited numbers. It is estimated that only 216 were ever produced—20 in 1967, 80 in '68 and 116 in '69. These numbers comprised a minuscule percentage of total Corvette production, but they were sufficient to bring widespread awareness of the awesome power of the L-88. Conversely, only *two* ZL-1 Corvettes were ever produced by Chevrolet and sold to the public. (A few others, the precise number is unknown, were used as magazine test cars, but they were either disassembled or destroyed; they disappeared following the press sessions. One of the 1969 ZL-1 test cars was actually a 1968 model that had previously seen service as a research and development vehicle.) Among Corvette enthusiasts the ZL-1 enjoys a legendary reputation, but outside of this coterie of aficionados, the option is virtually unknown.

Reduced to its most simplistic form, the ZL-1 can be described as an L-88 with an aluminum cylinder block. It has been written that $3,000, the cost of the ZL-1 option, was a rather steep price to pay for a reduction of 100 pounds of engine weight, but in point of fact, there were several other differences between the L-88 and ZL-1: Connecting rods were more substantial, exhaust ports were larger as were exhaust valves, the intake port shape was improved and the camshaft lifted the valves higher but didn't keep them open quite as long. Perhaps most important, construction of all ZL-1 engines (they were also available over-the-counter and in Camaros) took

Behind the Wheel

I depress the clutch pedal, check to ensure that the gear shift lever is in neutral, reach for the ignition key and turn it. The entire operation has a very familiar feel to it as well it should — I've logged well over 100,000 miles in a 1969 Corvette. But when the engine roars to life — and that's precisely what it does, roar — I instantly become aware that this is a whole new ball game. The tach needle is swinging between 1,500 and 1,700 rpm, but the engine is balky. It clearly does not want to run, reminding me of myself in the morning, before my first cup of coffee. As heat builds within it, the engine smooths out somewhat, but it's still apparent that at these revs it is a race horse being reined in.

The cacophony of all this reluctant internal combustion pervades the cockpit; other cars have authoritative exhaust sound, this one is Hitler raving through a megaphone. The side pipes were apparently designed to route exhaust out of the engine, not to silence it. But the exhaust notes are all I will hear; when the ZL-1 option was specified, a radio was considered frivolously irrelevant — one was not afforded the luxury of ordering one.

As I attempt to ease away from the curb — bump and grind is more like it — the engine still protests, although it does smooth out as the tach needle passes the 3,000 rpm mark. But now there's another banshee howling from beneath the floorboards. The mandatory M22 four-speed transmission, known as the "rock crusher" in the argot of Chevrolet racers, is making its presence known. In order to strengthen the transmission, the helix angle on the gears was altered from that of the standard Muncie four-speed. The trans may be strong, but it definitely isn't silent, especially in first and second gear.

Once the shift lever is placed in fourth, some of the racket subsides, and at speeds above 50 the engine is almost tractable. But it never really seems happy at part throttle. Even though it is constructed totally of Chevrolet parts, it is indeed a race engine. It was built to run at full throttle, and it only seems content when it is fulfilling its destiny.

The remainder of the car is in concert with the engine — nothing about it, save for the power brakes, makes it easy to drive on the highway. A bulge in the hood restricts forward visibility, the F-41 suspension is stiff enough to rattle the fillings out of your teeth, and when I'm unfortunate enough to be delayed at a stoplight, I must constantly eye the temperature gauge as the radiator is incapable of dissipating all the heat generated by the engine unless the car is in motion.

But after one blast down the highway at full throttle, I willingly forgive the ZL-1 for all its wickedness. With the accelerator pedal glued to the floor, the car transforms itself into a four-wheeled rocket. You feel as though you need a high-powered radio so that you can communicate with Mission Control.

The story of this particular ZL-1 Corvette is as convoluted as the car itself. Its present owner is Wayne Walker of Mechanicsville, Virginia. As Walker recounts the story, this particular car wasn't ordered through the dealer network but was taken directly from the assembly line by George Heberling who was then resident plant engineer of the St. Louis Corvette assembly facility. Heberling's purpose in ordering the car was to test the aluminum engine in everyday driving situations.

According to Walker's records, his ZL-1, bearing vehicle serial number 29219, rolled off the assembly line on June 30, 1969. Heberling drove the car for approximately 2,000 miles, but when he was transferred to another General Motors division, the car remained in St. Louis. Evidently, when Heberling wasn't using the car, it was occasionally used as a "loaner." Ralph Huseman, then a mechanic for GM's research and development department was temporarily assigned to the St. Louis facility toward the end of summer in 1969. As Huseman remembers his stint in St. Louis, "I did drive the car, along with another guy, back and forth to the hotel room — which didn't take very long." Huseman also recalls that in extra-curricular activities, nothing on the streets of St. Louis could touch the ZL-1.

General Motors, feeling that the car would be difficult to sell because of its $10,000 sticker price, circulated a memo through its dealer network in an effort to locate a buyer. At least 10 dealers responded, but for reasons unknown, Hechler Chevrolet was selected, and in November of 1969, car arrived in Richmond, Virginia. It was during the transfer operation that Jerry Lineback, at the time operations manager of Anchor Motor Freight Lines, became aware of the car. Being a Corvette enthusiast, Lineback realized that the yellow ZL-1 was no ordinary Corvette, so he photocopied all the pertinent documents for his personal records.

With the price on the window sticker totalling over $10,000, there were a lot of dreamers, but few serious buyers. Ultimately, John Zagos, a high school friend of Walker's who had inherited a considerable amount of money, purchased the car from the dealer. He immediately set about terrorizing the streets of Richmond, but his reign of terror didn't last long; the engine dropped a valve during its first night out on the town. Subsequently, the engine was returned to the dealer for a "warranty adjustment" and at this point, the story takes a bizarre twist — the original short block disappeared from the dealership, its replacement was installed in a drag boat and the car itself, less engine, reposed beside a filling station for two years, accompanied by a "For Sale" sign. Finally, a 454-cubic-inch powerplant was installed, the car was sold back to Hechler and the once glorious ZL-1 was all but forgotten.

But not by Walker. In 1976, inspired by a magazine article about rare Corvettes, he decided to attempt to locate the infamous ZL-1 and after searching diligently, he found the car only two blocks from his office. He immediately purchased it and through Zagos he also acquired some of the original engine pieces (carburetor, smog pump, air cleaner bottom) and the original "For Sale" ad run by Hechler Chevrolet in a local newspaper. But the search for the original block was considerably more difficult. Wayne was beginning to feel as though the situation was hopeless when a drag racer contacted him and stated he had the piece in question. Twenty-two hundred dollars later, Walker was the proud owner of the original block and an assortment of spare engine parts.

With all the necessary pieces in hand, Wayne began a serious restoration effort. "I felt as though I *had* to do a first class restoration — only two ZL-1s were ever built, but this is the only one that's properly documented. The other one is still around, but I don't believe it's original. That's just my opinion, but if you have such a car, you're going to find *something* to prove it. As yet, that hasn't happened."

After having the engine rebuilt and dyno tested, Walker restored the frame and undercarriage to original factory specifications and then took the entire car to Ken and Gary Nabers in Houston, Texas, for a concours quality paint job. The ZL-1 was finally returned to its original state of glory in June 1981 and with the paint barely dry, it was taken to the Bloomington Corvette Coral (the most prestigious of all Corvette shows) where it was judged best in class. A fitting tribute to the rarest of all Corvettes.

place in Chevrolet's engine manufacturing facility in Tonawanda, New York. The blocks, cast of 356 T-6 aluminum alloy, were machined on special tape-controlled machines and the engines were specially balanced and assembled with the care and cleanliness that is normally reserved for hospital operating rooms. The engines were subsequently dynamometer tested prior to shipment.

It paid off in performance—a ZL-1 prepared for road racing and fitted with a 3.70:1 rear-axle ratio blasted through the standing start/quarter mile in 12.1 seconds, reaching a top speed of 116 miles per hour. With a car modified specifically for drag racing, elapsed time dropped to 10.9 seconds and speed rose to 130 miles per hour.

In spite of all its power and glory, the ZL-1 Corvette has virtually no racing accolades surrounding it. This is a rather curious situation because quite a few Corvettes with aluminum engines did appear at race tracks across the nation. But these cars had either begun life with a cast-iron cylinder block, or had been built specifically as race cars. In the latter instance, the vehicles were pulled from the assembly line prior to completion, since they would be extensively reworked or gutted for use in other than Production class competition. As such, a production order form was never completed; from a General Motors documentation standpoint, these cars never existed.

In point of fact, the ZL-1 Corvette appears to have been created primarily for publicity purposes, a role in which it had unqualified success—there wasn't an automotive journalist to be found who didn't raid the dictionary in search of superlatives to describe the car's ability to accelerate. ᧶

Acknowledgments and Bibliography

Corvette: America's Star-Spangled Sports Car, by Karl Ludvigsen; Road & Track, various issues 1965-1969; Vette Vues magazine, various issues 1975-1980; Corvette News, various issues. Special thanks to Wayne Walker, Mechanicsville, Virginia; Ken and Gary Nabers, Houston, Texas; Bob Fitch, Houston, Texas; Anyone I Forgot; Theirtown, USA.

Voracious Vette

Cruising in the fast lane
behind the wheel of a 1970 LT-1 Corvette

by Richard Prince
photography by Robert Gross

   Originally published in Special Interest Autos #173, Sept.-Oct. 1999

A S the turbulent 1960s turned into the inflationary 1970s, the golden age of Detroit muscle cars was beginning to wind down. Overpaid and underworked Washington bureaucrats, incredibly greedy insurance industry executives, and well meaning but ignorant safety advocates formed a powerful alliance that effectively legislated high-performance cars out of existence within a few short years. But before these people could complete their stranglehold on automotive excitement, Zora Duntov and his compatriots at Chevrolet Engineering had one final trick up their collective sleeves. It was a high revving small-block engine labeled as option LT-1, and it became an instant legend when introduced in 1970.

The LT-1 was available in a variety of Chevrolet products, including of course the Corvette. At a cost of $447.60, which was $157.95 more than the optional LS-5 454 engine, the LT-1 was not exactly an inexpensive addition. This, in part, explains why only 1,287 Corvette purchasers, out of the 17,316 Corvettes built that year, checked off the LT-1 option on their 1970 order sheets.

What exactly did those 1,287 buyers get for their money? In short, they got one of the greatest all around driving experiences money could buy in 1970. If you are wondering exactly what it feels like to put an LT-1 Corvette through its paces, you're in luck as *SIA* takes you along for this comprehensive drive-Report.

Whether you've never sat in a 1968-82 Corvette before, or have driven hundreds of them, the feeling is always the same when you first get in. You sit down, really down. As in low to the ground. The sensation of being barely above the ground is accentuated by the encapsulating quality of the passenger compartment. If you are small of stature you're merely surrounded by the inside of the car. If you're a large person you practically wear the interior.

This feeling is definitely not for the claustrophobic among us. For those not afflicted with this phobia, including myself, the feeling is actually quite delightful. I feel much closer to the car than I do at the helm of something more spacious, and feel as though the car is an extension of my body.

Corvettes have had individual seats (I dare not call them buckets for reasons that anyone who ever sat in an early "solid axle" Corvette will recognize immediately) since the marque's inception in 1953. And while the seats improved practically every year and were always better than what was bolted into the vast majority of other cars of the same vintage, they still leave a lot to be desired by today's standards. In the absence of any kind of lateral supports, the only thing that keeps occupants

Large rectangular chrome exhaust tips fitted only on 1970-72 Stingrays.

PROS & CONS

PROS
1-Powerful, high revving engine
2-Voluptuous body style
3-Low maintenance and repairs
4-Excellent parts supply

CONS
1-Harsh ride
2-Poor fit and finish
3-Priced beyond average enthusiast
4-Plethora of unreliable gizmos and gadgets

Potent, solid lifter 350-inch LT-1 small-block makes 370-horsepower at 6,000 rpm.

from being flung out of the seats during hard cornering is the center console and door panel, which are right there, practically rubbing against your legs.

Corvettes have always had comprehensive instrumentation, and the 1970 is no exception. Intelligent placement and legibility have at times been questionable, but the early Sharks (as 1968-82 Corvettes are called) actually get high marks in this department. The tach and speedometer are large, easy to read, and right there where you need them. A secondary cluster of instruments is off to the driver's right in a housing above the radio. This works fine for everything except the oil pressure gauge, whose importance should never be underestimated. All else being equal, I would prefer it closer to my eyes when I'm looking at the road. If they really wanted to, the designers could have spread the speedo and tach apart a little bit and placed the oil pressure gauge between them. But they didn't. And besides, it's a minor complaint rendered somewhat moot by the incredible reliability of Chevrolet's engine oiling system.

The steering wheel in our LT-1 is typical of 1960s and '70s era sporty cars. Its decisively thin rim is rather large in diameter relative to today's wheels. Personally, I like it. My hands fit the finger recesses rather nicely, and its relatively large diameter allows easy visual access to the aforementioned speedo and tach. The big ring also comes in handy when steering a Corvette not equipped with power assist, which was an option in Corvettes until it became standard in 1977.

Pedals are well sized and placed for most people driving in most situations. Heel-and-toe maneuvers are pretty close to impossible on cars with manual brakes because the brake pedal is so much higher than the accelerator. On those Corvettes with power assist brakes, the brake pedal-to-accelerator pedal distance is cut nearly in half, making heel-and-toe action possible for the particularly dexterous and/or big footed. All others need to do some engineering and fabrication to get the two pedals in sync.

The shifter design found in our 1970 LT-1 was first used in 1964 Corvettes. Over the years it has generally been maligned by the go-fast crowd as something close to pure junk. In fact, stock shifters were tied with stock rims in the race to see what got replaced with aftermarket pieces the fastest. In my many years of driving and racing vintage Corvettes I have never had a problem with the stock shifter design. Of course,

Unique LT-1/big-block hood and egg-crate pattern grille are very distinctive. Rare hubcaps were optional.

when they are broken or plain worn out they stink. But the same can be said for Hurst shifters, too. The 1963 and older Corvettes are a different story—their shifters do not inspire confidence and merit immediate replacement if aggressive driving is in the game plan.

After evaluating the necessities—steering wheel, pedals, shifter, and the like—you begin to notice all the "extras." It is fair to say that the interior of a 1970 Corvette resembles the inside of a fighter plane, complete with enough gadgets and gizmos to choke a Holstein! Some love all the switches, lights, buzzers, fiber optics, and other toys, while others despise them. Dennis Hulme, World Champion Formula I and Can Am driver, definitely fell into the latter category. Writing for *Sports Car Graphic* magazine in 1969, he had this to say about the car's interior; "Good Lord, have you ever seen so many gadgets. . . . There were lights and switches that would have put the London Electric Works to shame!"

Well, like the interior "details" or not,

This Daytona Yellow beauty is owned by long time Corvette enthusiast, Dino Paritis, a Systems Architect in New York City. As the car's third owner, Dino bought the Vette in lieu of an engagement ring that his girlfriend wanted. While we don't know what became of the girl, we do know that Dino has grown so attached to his Corvette that he fanatically maintains it in its original shorwoom condition.

The car is maintained by Island Muscle Cars, in Amityville, Long Island, a shop known for their show-winning restorations. As you can see, this exceptional Corvette still wears its original paint, tires, hoses and belts. But although this stunning LT-1 beauty isn't driven very much, when it does hit the road everyone notices it. "I love the lines on the car, especially the hood," Dino told us. And, as expected, he added, "I love the sound of the solid cam and the feel of the power."

you're settled comfortably in the seat, everything you need is within easy reach, and you're ready to see what an LT-1 Corvette can do. You make sure the shifter is in the neutral gate, pump the accelerator a couple of times, and then turn the ignition key. Nothing. Oh yeah, you need to step on and hold the clutch pedal to complete the starter motor circuit. Now your twist of the key sets events in motion. If the engine is in a proper state of tune and the carburetor is working as it was intended, two revolutions of the starter motor is all it takes to bring the potent 350-inch small-block to life.

And when an LT-1 comes to life a symphony of sound bursts forth. The exhaust has a deep rumble accentuated by a slight rumpety-rumpety-rumpety that results from the performance camshaft profile. Added to this of course is the steady click-and-tap of the solid lifter valve train, a hallmark of the LT-1. The solid lifters, in concert with a host of other high performance features, enable the engine to climb eagerly to its 6,500-

89

rpm redline. These other high-rpm components include a two-and-a-half-inch exhaust system, Delco transistor ignition, and a dual-feed 850 cfm Holley carburetor. The two-and-a-half-inch exhaust lets the LT-1 breathe better by virtue of low-restriction mufflers and pipes that are half an inch larger than the standard engine's two-inch system. Curiously, even though the LT-1 gets two-and-a-half-inch pipes it still uses the same two-inch exhaust manifolds as the base engine. The larger pipes are swaged down to fit the smaller manifolds.

Within two or three minutes, the engine coolant temperature comes up, and a quick flick of the accelerator deactivates the automatic choke and its accompanying fast idle. Engine rpm settles in around 750 rpm and the mechanical lifters grow quieter as most of their clearance is taken up by thermal expansion. In with the clutch, which by the way is remarkably user friendly in spite of its ample clamping power, and the shifter is manipulated into its first gear position. Ease out the clutch, apply a bit of throttle, and away you go.

If your ride is fitted with a 4.11:1 rear end gear ratio, as were many LT-1s, you have to exercise considerable restraint

Dual-feed 850 cfm Holley 4-barrel carburetor is stock, and sits atop aluminum intake manifold.

to prevent the car from leaping off the line and chirping the tires. A more highway friendly ratio, such as a 3.36:1, makes civilized starts easier. And it does so, I should add, without sacrificing all that much in the way of neck snapping acceleration. While the LT-1 is right at home in the upper rpm range, it still retains a remarkably broad torque curve. Even with high-speed rear gears, off the line enthusiasm is quite impressive. So we've launched the car in first gear and we're off and running. Faster than you can say "I simply love the scintillatingly sweet song of a solid lifter small-block," the rev counter has jumped way up and kissed the red line, signaling that it's time to find second gear.

How did the engine revs get up there so very quickly? Well, the ability of the LT-1 to climb through the rpm band with speed-of-light quickness is one of the attributes that makes this engine so special. Its 370-horsepower and 380 foot pounds of torque ratings are impressive enough, but they don't tell the full story. An LT-1 Corvette will actually out accelerate lighter and more powerful vehicles that look, on paper at least, faster. Its fuel curve, ignition curve, and most importantly, its camshaft profile, are what make this remarkable engine such a rapid revver.

Needing to engage gear number two, you push the clutch in, pull the shifter back, and let the clutch back out in one seamless motion. This all happens very quickly, but if you want to speed it up further that can be accomplished without too much trouble. You just need to perform a linkage adjustment. The previously praised stock shifter has two linkage settings. It came from the factory set for long throws but can be adjusted to function with short throws. The short-throw settings suit my taste, not because it makes me feel like Racer X, but because it simply feels better. In a car where just about everything is quick

RESTORING AN LT-1 CORVETTE

Collector interest in 1970–72 LT-1 Corvettes seems to grow continuously stronger, and restoration of these cars is a very popular undertaking. Because of this, the aftermarket parts industry supplies the vast majority of parts needed to accomplish a detailed, correct restoration.

The overwhelming majority of parts in an LT-1 Corvette interchange with other Corvettes of the same period. Replacement body panels, suspension, steering, and brake parts, interior trim items, exterior chrome and trim, body glass, weather-stripping, and chassis parts are all readily available.

Most chassis and drivetrain parts found underneath a 1970–72 Corvette are virtually identical to the pieces used in many other year Corvettes. The same disc brake system was used from 1965–82, the complete front and rear suspension assemblies and steering linkage were largely unchanged from 1963–82, the differential is interchangeable from 1963–79, and so on. This makes it relatively easy and inexpensive to replace what's missing and fix what's broken.

While 98 percent of the parts needed to restore a 1970–72 Corvette are only a phone call away, there are a handful of items that are more difficult to locate. For example, you will have a devil of a time trying to find a correct dated and numbered carburetor for a 1970 equipped with an LT-1 engine and option NA9. This option was a California-only emissions package that was required on all cars sold new in that state. Part of the package was an evaporative emissions control solenoid attached to the fuel system. Cars so equipped had a unique carburetor that is quite difficult to find.

Other difficult to find parts include: 100 percent correct mufflers (originals were supplied by Walker and differ in a number of subtle ways from the best available reproductions); Air Injection Reactor Systems (the AIR pumps and other parts are not reproduced and many originals quickly found their way into the trash can when the cars were still new); and some of the pieces that went into the road racing ZR-1 option package.

In addition to the general availability of the vast majority of needed parts, there are other considerations that facilitate restoration of a 1970–72 Corvette. Excruciatingly detailed information about how the cars were originally built and equipped, right down to every last part number and date code, is available. There is a very strong support network of clubs that disseminate this information and assist restoration efforts in general.

Also, the nature of the cars themselves makes their restoration easier than many other vehicles. Obviously, with fiberglass body panels, body rot is never a problem. Body-on-frame construction makes it pretty straightforward to remove the body to thoroughly restore the underpinnings. And though the cars have more than a fair share of gizmos and gadgets, they were created in an era when sound mechanical and common sense still went pretty far in diagnosing and solving problems. In other words, you don't need a Ph.D. in electrical engineering or computer science to fix these cars.

All 1970-72 Corvettes featured these stylish egg-crate pattern side fender grilles.

and to the point, a long-throw shifter seems inexcusably out of place. In another car it would likely feel quite appropriate, but in a Corvette it feels as though I'm churning butter.

So what does it really feel like to accelerate an LT-1 enthusiastically through all four forward gears? It's 98 percent exhilaration mixed with two percent apprehension. The exhilaration part is easy to understand, but what about the apprehension? Well, a 1970 Corvette is not the most predictable of creatures, particularly when shod with lousy, skinny OEM-style bias-ply tires. There's always the danger that the rear tires will break loose and the whole car will get squirrelly. For those not used to brute force delivered in a somewhat crude package, this apprehension can be exacerbated by the totality of the sensory experience one has when zooming in an early '70s Corvette. Let's start with what you see. Front visibility is poor to begin with, owing to the low seating position, high fender peaks, and long nose. And it gets noticeably worse when the car is under hard acceleration because the front-end lifts precipitously. Then there's the noise. The racket of solid lifters, the pop of 11:1 compression, the smack of forged aluminum pistons, it all adds up to a monumental roar of power. In fact, the ferocious growl of the engine and drivetrain gets so overwhelming that it actually obscures the groans and rattles inherent to even the tightest of '70 Corvettes.

Now you know what the raw, unbridled acceleration of an LT-1 Corvette feels like. What about the remainder of the driving experience? After all, Corvettes are supposed to be sports cars and well-balanced GT cars as well as muscle cars.

'The racket of solid lifters, the pop of 11:1 compression, the smack of forged aluminum pistons, it all adds up to a monumental roar of power.'

This 1970 Corvette, like all Corvettes since 1965, stops as well as it goes. The secret is the four-wheel disc brake setup that became standard issue in '65. Four-piston calipers clamping down on 11.7-inch-diameter vented rotors do a commendable job of dissipating the kinetic energy harbored in a 3,500-pound object moving forward at one hundred or more miles per hour.

specifications

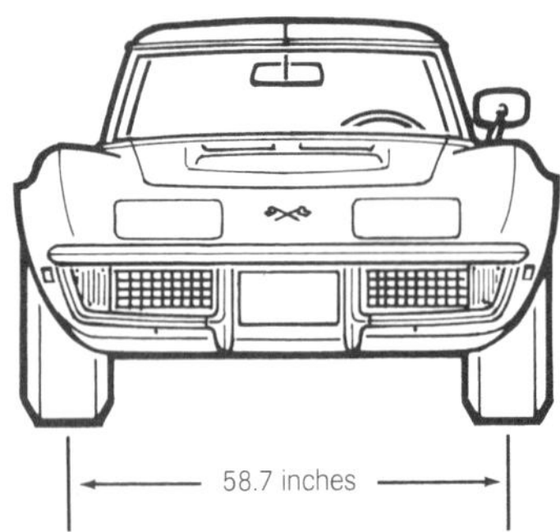

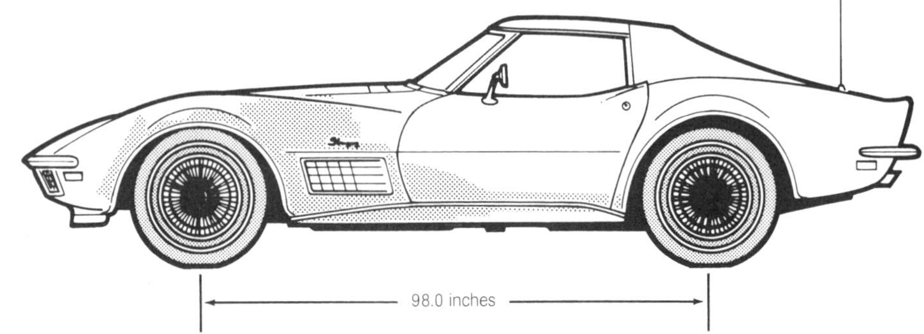

1970 Corvette LT-1

Price $5,192

Std. equip. included Turbo-Fire 350/270-horsepower V-8, dual exhaust, 4-wheel disc brakes, 4-wheel independent suspension, high-back bucket seats, full instrumentation

Options on dR car LT-1 engine ($447.60); J50

Price as equipped $5,850.30

ENGINE

Type	V-8
Bore x stroke	4.00 inches x 3.48 inches
Displacement	350 cubic inches
Compression ratio	11.0:1
Horsepower @ rpm	370 @ 6,000
Torque @ rpm	380 @ 4,000
Valve gear	Overhead valve, rocker arms, push rods
Valve lifters	Solid Lifters
Main bearings	5
Induction system	Holley 4-bbl on aluminum intake
Fuel system	Mechanical pump
Lubrication system	Pressure, gear type pump
Cooling system	Pressure, centrifugal pump
Exhaust system	Cast iron manifolds, 4 into 1, dual
Electrical system	12-volt

TRANSMISSION

Type	4-speed manual
Ratios: 1st	2.20:1
2nd	1.64:1
3rd	1.27:1
4th	1.00:1

DIFFERENTIAL

Type	Hypoid, limited-slip
Ratio	4.11:1

STEERING

Type	Recirculating ball with hydraulic assist
Turns lock-to-lock	3.4
Overall ratio	20.2:1
Turning circle	39.0 feet

BRAKES

Type	4-wheel disc with vacuum servo
Front	11.7 inches, diameter vented disc
Rear	11.7 inches, diameter vented disc
Swept area	461.2 square inches
Parking brake	Mechanical, on rear drums

CHASSIS & BODY

Construction	Body on steel ladder frame
Body	Fiberglass over steel subframe
Body style	2-seat coupe

SUSPENSION

Front	Independent, upper and lower control arms, coil springs, link-type anti-roll bar
Rear	Independent, trailing arms, transverse leaf spring
Shock absorbers	Delco tube shocks
Tires	F70 x 15
Wheels	Stamped steel disc, 15 x 8

WEIGHTS AND MEASURES

Wheelbase	98.0 inches
Overall length	182.5 inches
Overall width	69.0 inches
Overall height	47.4 inches
Front track	58.7 inches
Rear track	59.4 inches
Ground clearance	4.5 inches
Shipping weight	3,153 pounds
Weight as tested	Approximately 3,550 pounds
Distribution front/rear	49%/51%

CAPACITIES

Crankcase	5 quarts (plus 1 quart for filter)
Cooling system	18 quarts
Fuel tank	18 gallons
Transmission	2.5 pints
Differential	3 3/4 pints

CALCULATED DATA

Horsepower per c.i.d.	1.06
Weight per hp	8.52 pounds per hp
Lb./sq. in. brakes	7.22 pounds
Stroke/bore ratio	.87:1

Stopping power is especially impressive in Corvettes equipped with power brakes, as our feature car is. Whether powered or not, the actual braking system at all four wheels is the same. Nonetheless, without the vacuum assist a considerable pedal effort is called for and it feels as though the car doesn't stop as well. While I can find no fault with the power and braking capability of this 1970 LT-1, the same can not be said for the third side of the performance triangle, its handling.

It's not that the car's handling is awful, because it's not. In fact, compared with most other cars available in 1970 it is quite good. And compared with 454-powered Corvettes of the same

era it is markedly better. What the LT-1 gave up in horsepower to the big-block was more than made up for by the fact that it weighed over one hundred pounds less than the larger engined car. In spite of the fact that it compares very favorably with its contemporaries, the 1970 Corvette's handling is somewhat less than perfect. Almost since its inception, the Corvette has been a hybrid of sorts. It's part muscle car and part sports car. Well, in the muscle car arena it has known few peers. In the sports car department however, it has often been bested by a host of other, purer machines.

Part of the problem is the car's weight. Your standard issue, road ready 1970

160-mph speedometer is very optimistic.

Shifter can be adjusted for short throws.

LT-1 tips the scales at about 3,550 pounds. It is simply not feasible to get a car of that mass to handle as nimbly as one weighing half a ton less. Another part of the problem is tires. 1970 Corvettes came with either Goodyear Wide Treads or Firestone Wide Ovals sized at F70-15. Again, it is not realistic to expect a two-and-three-quarter ton car riding on bias ply tires having six-inch wide treads to handle superbly. The tires tend to be jittery, following the vagaries of the road surface. And understeer can be quite pronounced at times. If spirited driving is your cup of tea, the most immediately available tool for curing the innate understeer is directly beneath your right foot. Judicious application of the throttle can be very effective at pointing the nose in the direction you wanted it to head for to begin with.

A more time consuming but at times worthwhile solution to the Corvette's less than perfect handling involves modifying the suspension in some very basic ways. Polyurethane bushings can substitute for the stock rubber pieces throughout the undercarriage. Stiffer springs in an almost infinite range of ratings are easily substituted for the originals. Ditto for fatter anti-roll bars, better shock absorbers, and a variety of other bits and pieces attached to the chassis. And of course, there are those skinny bias-ply tires. Replacing them with a set of chubbier, stickier modern high performance radials is probably the single most effective thing you can do to improve the car's handling characteristics. In spite of less than perfect handling traits, a good, long, uninhibited drive in a 1970 LT-1 Corvette is still an invigorating experience. It brings out the car's many strengths as well as its few weaknesses.

'A 1970 Corvette is not the most predictable of creatures, particularly when shod with lousy, skinny OEM-style bias-ply tires.'

THE COMPETITION

No car exists in a vacuum, and to fully appreciate a vehicle's strengths and weaknesses it is important to understand the other cars in the marketplace it was competing with.

As discussed in the text, the Corvette has always been a hybrid of sorts, part muscle car, part sports car, and part grand touring car. As such, 1970-72 LT-1s had no real direct competitors because there were no other cars that crossed all three lines the way the Corvettes did.

Of course, there were numerous sports cars on the market. They included the near exotic and exotic, like the 911 Porsche, Jaguar XKE, and 365 GTB/4 Ferrari. They also included the traditional, like the Triumph TR6 and Spitfire, MG Midget, and Fiat 124 Sport Spyder.

There were also plenty of muscle and grand touring cars offered in the early 1970s. Big-block Mustangs, Hemi-powered Chryslers, and the like provided plenty of pure muscle. Well balanced cars like the BMW 2002 and 2800 CS, as well as the Alfa Romeo 1750 GTV, offered those seeking a GT car something to consider.

Oddly enough, the car that definitely came closest to the LT-1 Corvette in terms of all around performance, and very well may have been its stiffest competition in the sales arena, was the Z/28 Camaro. While the Z/28 Camaro was not a sports car, its handling was excellent. And with an LT-1 of its own under the hood, its acceleration and top speed were virtually identical to that of its Corvette sister.

While the Camaro has never had the same animal allure as the Corvette, their extremely close performance in the early 1970s did make them competitors. And with a sticker price that rounded off to roughly $1,700 less than a comparably equipped Corvette, the Z/28 did enjoy a strong advantage in terms of bang for the buck.

WHAT'S IT WORTH?

With most Corvettes, originality affects value. If the engine ID numbers match the chassis ID numbers, then the Corvette's value will be considerably more than a non-matching numbers car. So, too, will the car's overall condition. For a sampling of asking prices as listed in *Hemmings Motor News*, the following prices reflect the state of the LT-1 market during June and July 1999.

1970 LT-1 Coupe, M21, matching drivetrain, California car until 3/97, black with black leather, clean, straight, Survivor, 82K, runs awesome, $17,900.

1970 LT-1 Coupe, 4-speed, numbers match, Bridgehampton blue, black interior, 69K, documented body-off restoration, mechanically perfect, $29,500.

1970 LT-1 Coupe, 48K, Daytona Yellow, black comfort weave, 3.70 posi, completely original and unrestored, 96-point NCRS Top Flight award, $32,000.

All cars, including Corvettes and others that were engineered for driving enthusiasts, are inevitably a compromise among numerous competing interests. As I said previously, Corvettes have always been a hybrid, never a pure muscle car, a pure sports car, or a pure grand touring car. Engineers, designers, bean counters, marketing gurus, and a gaggle of others all got their turn to stir the pot when it came to creating the car. And in Chevrolet's recipe for the LT-1 Corvette, two teaspoons of handling and finesse were mixed with four teaspoons of tire scorching, high revving horsepower. If you prefer four teaspoons of civility and handling prowess and only two teaspoons of get-up-and-go, then an LT-1 Corvette is not the meal for you. If you like your muscle/sports/GT machines with a heavier measure of muscle, however, you'll find this car irresistibly delicious.

While the focus of our Corvette driving experience has been what the engine, drivetrain, and underpinnings all feel like, it is also important to consider what the aesthetics of the car contribute

The Stingray's low-slung cockpit is very comfortable even for drivers taller than 6'-2".

REPAIR COSTS

Prices include parts & labor

1–Tune-up: $200
Add 1/2 hour labor if the car has air conditioning, which makes it more difficult to change spark plugs (1972 was the only year a/c was available with an LT-1 engine in a Corvette.)
Deduct 1/2 hour if the car does not have ignition shielding.

2–Stock engine rebuild: $2,500
Add $650 to remove and reinstall the engine in the car.
Add another $250 for incidentals like antifreeze, hoses, belts, engine mounts, exhaust manifold studs, and so on.

3–Transmission rebuild: $250-$700,
depending upon what parts are needed. Parts price can increase by 50%-75% for optional M-22 transmission rebuild.

4–Clutch replacement: $650

5–Suspension overhaul: $1,800
Add $400 per side for labor and parts to rebuild the rear wheel bearing assemblies and trailing arms.

6–Brakes front and rear: $750,
includes replacement calipers with stainless steel sleeves, new pads, hoses, short rear hard lines, and hardware.
Add $300 to replace four rotors with new rotors.
Add 1/2 hour labor if rear rotor retention rivets need to be drilled out to release rotors for machining.
Add 6 hours labor if old calipers need to be removed and renewed with new pistons, springs, and seals.
Deduct $350 for parts and 2 hours labor if calipers don't need to be replaced with sleeved units.

PRICE GUIDE

As per N.A.D.A. Appraisal Guide

Model	Low	Avg.	High
1970	$11,900	$19,125	$29,550
1971	$ 9,150	$13,575	$21,325
1972	$ 9,250	$13,775	$21,425

to the overall package. The Shark body style was first seen as a one-off show car in April 1965 at the New York International Auto Show. Dubbed Mako Shark II, it was one of numerous design/engineering concepts being considered for the next generation production car. In modified form it beat out all the other concept vehicles and became the 1968 Corvette. Though continuously tweaked over time, the essential form of the Mako Shark II-inspired '68 body stayed unchanged through the 1982 model year. This 15-year run makes it the longest lasting Corvette design in the 46-year history of the marque.

Corvettes built from 1968 through '72 are sometimes called chrome-bumper Sharks to distinguish them from the subsequent rubber bumper Sharks. As you would suspect, the chrome-bumper Sharks still wore the chrome bumpers that were a Corvette staple since 1953. 1973 models had a urethane front bumper and chrome rear bumpers, making it something of a hybrid. Chrome bumper Sharks are particularly popular with collectors today in large part because of the fore and aft chrome. They add a dash of flash to the cars and integrate the classic look of previous generation Corvettes with the more modern look of the later, rubber bumper

Sharks. In addition to the chrome bumpers front and rear, which differentiate 1970-72 Sharks from later Corvettes, the cars are distinguished from previous models by integrated fender flares and styling details.

The 1968 and '69 Corvettes certainly looked beautiful, but their bodies were prone to stone chipping immediately behind the wheel openings because the fenders and quarters rolled under and inboard of the tires. This problem was addressed beginning in 1970 with the inclusion of molded-in fender flares behind the wheels at all four corners. Besides protecting the paint, these flares give the cars a wider, more aggressive stance. Other styling features that distinguish the 1970-72 Corvettes are the vacuum actuated windshield wiper door and unique LT-1/big-block hood, both of which were eliminated in 1973. Other design elements unique to the 1970-72 models are the egg crate pattern front and side fender grilles, and the large rectangular exhaust tips.

All of the 1970-72s, and in fact all of the 1968-82 Shark Corvettes, feature styling unlike anything else in the world. This, combined with their outstanding performance on the road, has made them extremely popular with collectors in recent years. Of course, the early chrome bumper cars, especially ones equipped with high performance options like the featured LT-1, are especially sought after. As I said earlier, if you like your muscle/sports/GT machines with a heavy measure of muscle mixed in with excellent stopping power and agile handling, you'll find this car irresistibly delicious. ✍

Notes

Notes